T0161064

PRAISE FOR *COMPASSIONARIES*

David Crocker has been reading my mail. His call to embrace the stewardship of our life and become *Compassionaries* is Jesus-centered and desperately needed if the American church is going to have a future. Becoming a compassionary is the crucial antidote to the diseases of affluenza, self-absorption and irrelevance that haunt our churches.
　　—Bill Wilson, Director, The Center for Healthy
　　Churches

David Crocker passionately reminds us that Jesus calls each of us to live our daily lives as missionaries with love and service for others. He beautifully illustrates how true mission work is not reserved for a select few nor limited to international travel. With humble sacrificial service, we find purpose, extend true hope and can actually change the world.
　　—Mark H. Maxwell, author of *Networking Kills:*
　　Success Through Serving

As a Lutheran Pastor for 42 years and an ELCA Bishop for 12 years, I have never before read such a compelling engaging book about the power of serving others. I personally have witnessed the releasing of life-giving compassion touching and blessing the lives of others. This book is a practical hope filled guide about the significance of one's daily life becoming an arena of serving God and one's neighbors. I highly recommend it.

—Rev. Herman Yoos, retired Bishop of the South Carolina Synod of Lutheran Churches (ELCA)

Service to others is what God uses to change people and change the world. Service may be the greatest agent of change that there is. *Compassionaries* by David Crocker is a great book about the need for and value of service to others!

—Richard Brunson, Executive Director, North Carolina Baptists on Missions

Through his experiences and observations, David Crocker inspires us to cultivate a mindset of serving others. Whether at work, at home, or in our communities, we have endless opportunities to serve others in a way that encourages them and leaves them feeling loved. That kind of love is the central principle of our Christian faith.

—Cheryl Batchelder, author of *Dare to Serve: How to Drive Superior Results by Serving Others*

COMPASSIONARIES

Unleash the Power of Serving

COMPASSIONARIES

Unleash the Power of Serving

David W. Crocker

Carpenter's Son Publishing

Compassionaries: Unleash the Power of Serving

© 2021 by David Crocker

All rights reserved. No part of this book may be reproduced or transmitted in
any form or by any means, electronic or mechanical, including photocopying,
recording or by any information storage and retrieval system, without permission in writing from the copyright owner.

Published by Carpenter's Son Publishing, Franklin, Tennessee

Published in association with Larry Carpenter
of Christian Book Services, LLC
www.christianbookservices.com

Scripture quotations marked (NIV) are taken from the Holy Bible, New
International Version®, NIV®. Copyright © 1973, 1978, 1984, 2011 by Biblica,
Inc.™ Used by permission of Zondervan. All rights reserved worldwide. www.
zondervan.com The "NIV" and "New International Version" are trademarks
registered in the United States Patent and Trademark Office by Biblica, Inc.™

Cover design by Brenna Lundy

Interior design by Suzanne Lawing

Printed in the United States of America

978-1-952025-86-0

This book is dedicated to my parents,
Charles and Mae Crocker,
who have lived a very long life serving others,
and who have never failed to believe in
me and use every opportunity to encourage
me in every endeavor I undertake,

and

To my wife, Brenda, whose belief in me
and faithful encouragement of my work
has sustained me in good times and bad
and whose love I cherish more than I can say.

Compassionary: \kum-ˈpa-shen-er-ee\ n   1. Compound word: compassion and missionary. 2. One who is inspired to show compassion to people in need and change the world for the better. 3. One sent to care for those who cannot provide for themselves: missionary-like at inspiring others to serve as well. 4. A change agent emboldened to make a difference, serving beyond responsibilities to family and work to give help and hope to the least, the lonely and the lost.

CONTENTS

PART FOUR

INTRODUCTION

A *Peanuts* comic strip shows Linus watching his favorite TV show when Lucy comes in and promptly changes the channel to what she wants to watch. Linus says, "What makes you think you can walk in here and change the channel like you own the place?" Lucy balls up her fist and says, "These five fingers, that's what. Individually, they aren't much, but when I put them together they become a force to be reckoned with." Linus says meekly, "Okay." In the final frame of the strip, Linus looks at his own hand and says, "Why can't you guys work together like that?"

We have in our hands a force to be reckoned with, not as Lucy intends, but a force nevertheless. I am convinced each and every person has available to him a power capable of far more than ever imagined. I'm not talking about a tool or weapon or *any* object but our hands themselves--or ourselves. When we serve others, we tap into a power that exceeds our knowledge or expectations.

After years of observing what serving others does—both for the person serving and for those being served—I was moved to write this book. I have found that serving others is a powerful force capable of transforming our lives and the lives of those we serve. Serving has the power to give hope to the hopeless, joy to the depressed, and unity to the divided. It has the power to make things happen for good—for individuals and families and churches and communities, perhaps for the world. Like many of you, I have served others in lots of ways without thinking much about what I was doing and without realizing the transformational power of serving. But the light has dawned! Like an inventor who has labored for years to discover what works and suddenly it shows up as plain as day, I have come to see how powerful serving others can be and how much our world desperately needs this power implemented as widely as possible.

Now, I want to share all this with everyone who will listen. I am like the child who just learned how to read or ride a bicycle and can't wait to tell everyone about it. I want as many people as possible to discover the joys of serving, and I want as many people in need as possible to receive the help and hope they so earnestly desire. Furthermore, I am convinced serving can revive the best of what it means to be community.

While I have been deeply engaged in serving from a faith perspective, I believe the principles of serving set forth in this book apply to everyone whether believer or not. In fact, I have tried to write in such a way as to appeal to people who might never consider serving with a church group or for reasons that have nothing to do with a relationship with God. This does not mean I have abandoned my own faith perspective, just that the world is bigger, and the needs are greater than will be met by the church.

The purpose of this book is to inspire you to think deeply about serving and to give yourself to serving others. This comes at a unique time for our nation. As I write, we can see light at the end of the COVID tunnel. Despite news of variant strains of the virus and slowing rates of vaccinations, we hear official announcements about removing restrictions on social interactions we have endured for more than a year. What's interesting is that while we have been restricted in what we can do, many people have responded by serving more than they have in the past. One survey in May, 2021, says 52 percent of Americans have volunteered in some capacity during the pandemic and many indicate they will continue.

So, the time is right for a book about serving. *Compassionaries* says every person has a role to play in serving. Everyone--young or old, strong or disabled, educated or not, rich or poor—can serve. Furthermore, the more people who take up serving as a lifestyle the better our communities and world will be. Can you imagine what it would look like if everyone adopted a serving attitude? What if serving were to become as common as watching television or keeping up with our favorite sports teams or, dare I say it, keeping up with Facebook or Twitter?

A word about the term compassionaries. It is a combination of "compassion" and "missionaries." It is my word to describe people who are missionary-like in their practice and proclamation of compassion. The term is meant to serve as a word picture of serving so that its use both raises curiosity and inspires the spread of compassion for people in need.

The book is divided into four parts. The first defines serving as helping a person in need as opposed to some of the other uses of the term and leans into the example of Jesus as the Model Servant. The second examines the benefits of serving for individuals who serve and those being served as well as the larger community. The third takes an in-depth look at the characteristics of those who serve others and offers practical steps a person can take to find her place in serving. And the fourth deals with some of the challenges of serving and wraps up with a clarion call to help start a serving movement that has the potential to change the world.

A strong believer in the power of story, I have included several stand-alone, extended stories of people I know who have exemplified what it means to be a compassionary. Each one exhibits a different aspect of serving and, I trust, adds to the persuasiveness of the book's message.

What will you get from reading this book? You will learn how serving enhances your own mental health, how it gives those being served more than they realize, and how it transforms their community. You will be guided in a practical process of discovery of your experiences and passions, pointing you to places of service for which you are best suited. Finally, you will gain an understanding of those issues that make some people hesitant to serve and how to overcome them. *Compassionaries* comes with a warning: If you don't want to serve, don't read this book.

PART ONE

Chapter One

WHY THIS? WHY NOW? WHY ME?

*Life is too short not to create, not to love, and not to lend a
helping hand to our brothers and sisters.*
--MARTIN LUTHER KING, JR.

Emily is eleven years old, but she's not your typical eleven-
year-old, absorbed in gaining the acceptance of her peers as
she transitions from childhood into adolescence. Emily is
focused on helping others. Recently, she and her friend Abby
collected almost two thousand pairs of shoes for homeless
children in nearby Charlotte, North Carolina, an impressive
accomplishment for anyone, much less two eleven-year-old
girls.

Here's how it happened. Emily became concerned about
the needs of some children around her and did her own research into their needs. She discovered that Charlotte and
the surrounding area had as many as four thousand homeless
children and that one of their biggest needs was shoes. So, she
set out to provide shoes by founding a tiny organization she

named "Soles for Kids Shoe Drive". Not one to think too small, she set a goal of collecting a thousand pairs of shoes in her first Shoe Drive. She applied for a $500 grant from Youth Service America and the Disney Summer Service Program. The application required Emily to write an essay describing the need she found and how she planned to meet that need. Her heartfelt essay did the trick and she was awarded the grant. Her first task in getting Soles for Kids up and running was to clean out the shoe departments of two nearby WalMart stores.

As word of Emily's project spread, others got involved—specifically, Verizon Wireless and the Charlotte Checkers Hockey Team. By the time Emily and her project partners completed the Soles for Kids Shoe Drive, they had collected and delivered 1898 pairs of shoes to local homeless shelters! And Emily isn't done yet. Reflecting on her experience, Emily says, "I want to help more kids get out there, start their own projects and inspire more kids at an early age."[1] Emily saw a need and met it. She is a compassionary.

Millard Fuller's story is one of the most impressive in recent times. Fuller was born in a sleepy little Alabama town. He studied law and with his partner, Morris Dees, who co-founded the Southern Poverty Law Center were also enormously successful entrepreneurs. They sold tractor cushions, rat poison, candy and toothbrushes, "and almost all of it made money," said Fuller. They tried to sell mistletoe but couldn't get enough to sell by shooting it out of trees. By age twenty-nine, Millard Fuller was a millionaire.

---

1 Accessed May 15, 2021. https://www.onlygood.tv/soles-for-kids-shoe-drive-2507466750.html

Success brought tension to his marriage and after long discussions, he and his wife, Linda, decided to sell everything they had and give away the proceeds. Soon, they moved to Americus, Georgia to join Koinonia Farm, a Christian commune founded by Clarence Jordan, a farmer and New Testament Greek scholar and author. Sustained by the community at Koinonia Farms and with their knowledge of economic success, the Fullers introduced the idea of providing affordable housing through no-interest loans and volunteer labor to people too poor to own their own homes through traditional means. This concept would become Habitat for Humanity. Habitat is now a household name. It has the respect of everyone, and every year involves tens of thousands of people in meeting the need of affordable housing for the poor. Personally, I count it a privilege to have helped in the building of about 10 Habitat homes. I believe in the concept so much that I once rode my bicycle from the mountains to the coast of North Carolina to raise money to build a Habitat house.

Millard Fuller saw a need and met it. More importantly, he had a vision that was much larger than himself, involving millions of others in solving one of the world's most persistent problems. He once told the Chicago *Tribune*, "We want to make shelter a matter of conscience. We want to make it socially, politically, morally and religiously unacceptable to have substandard housing and homelessness."[2] Millard and Linda Fuller were compassionaries.

---

2 Accessed May 15, 2021. Patricia Sullivan, https://www.washingtonpost.com/local/obituaries/millard-fuller-self-made-millionaire-who-founded-habitat-for-humanity-dies-at-74/2019/02/03/8fa60576-27dc-11e9-8eef-0d74f4bf0295_story.html .

Aubrey makes money building doll houses but he makes his living by caring for the poor. He began serving by filling his car with day-old bread and delivering it across the border in Tijuana, Mexico. It was a classic case of "one thing leads to another." Soon, he was filling a van, and before long (and this is the honest truth!), he was filling jumbo jets (747s and DC-10s) with food for Africa and Eastern Europe. A few years ago, he challenged his church to help him feed the hungry in Los Angeles and San Diego (no one can accuse him of thinking small). He said he had a hunch farmers in California would be willing to help, too. Soon, Aubrey found fresh vegetables and other nutritious foods available through local sources and continued his quest to feed hungry people in Southern California. Following his example and inspired by his enthusiasm, the church bought a diesel tractor and trailers. Today, they move at least 100,000 pounds of food a week.[3] Aubrey saw a need and met it. He is another compassionary.

I could go on and on with stories like these and I wouldn't get tired of sharing them and you wouldn't get tired of reading them. They inspire us and challenge us. They make us wish we could do something significant to help others. That is precisely the reason I am writing this book:

- To inspire people who are not serving to begin to serve

- To inspire people who are serving to serve more

- To educate readers about the principles of serving

- To help you find a place of service that fits you

---

3 Donald McCullough. *The Trivialization of God.* NavPress Publishing Group, Colorado Springs, CO, 1995, p. 149.

- To help you navigate your way through reasons for not serving and issues that come with serving

- To inspire a movement of serving that will become the norm and will transform communities

IS IT REALISTIC TO THINK JUST ANYONE CAN EMULATE THE PEOPLE IN THESE STORIES?

No and Yes. These are extraordinary stories which is one of the reasons they are so inspiring. None of these people set out to become famous or do something they thought might be inspirational or even noteworthy. Each one simply saw a need and did what they could to meet it... in a fairly small way... in the beginning. Only later, when their concepts of serving became known in their communities and beyond, when they gathered momentum and garnered more notoriety did any of these individuals become extraordinary. Each one saw a need and met a need. And, yes, anyone can emulate that plan.

Maybe it would help to see other examples of serving that have not made headlines, service that no one else even knows about. Somewhere today an observant onlooker will help an elderly person who is having difficulty getting groceries to her car and/or into her home. Somewhere today a teacher will take time to listen to a troubled student who is having problems at home and try to comfort him. Somewhere today a motorist will stop to change another motorist's flat tire because she doesn't have a clue how to do it herself, then both of them will go on their way.

I could go on, but you get the point. Small but not insignificant acts of serving others will take place unexpectedly and unnoticed today and tomorrow and pretty much every day. Each one is an incident of authentic serving—one person seeing a need and doing what he/she can do to meet that need. Each one is the result of one or more people being willing to get involved to help another person. For that moment, each one of those people is a compassionary.

So, here's a question: Why do some people get involved in serving and others do not? I hope every person reading this book will ask himself that question. The answer's not so simple as "Some people have the time and some do not," or "Some people are oriented that way while others are not."

Think for a moment about all that has happened in the weight-loss industry in recent years. An explosion of information about how we lose weight has resulted in a plethora of diets and the vast expansion of weight-loss psychology. As a result, more people than ever are involved in some sort of weight-loss program. More accurate knowledge about how we gain and lose weight has led to more people involved.

Visit your local bookstore and check out the self-help section. The number of topics, ranging from how-to books to parenting to meditation to personal finance and beyond, staggers our imagination. The vast amount of information on any topic is available at our fingertips via cellphones and I-pads, and podcast subscribers and Twitter followers number in the millions. More and more people are involved in seeking some sort of knowledge or information.

Why shouldn't we expect that knowledge about serving will yield more involvement in serving as well? I am not so naïve as to think providing more information about serving will completely close the gap between non-servers and servers, but perhaps it can move the needle at least a little.

AREN'T THERE PLENTY OF PEOPLE SERVING ALREADY?

Yes, many people are serving, especially now. The percentage of people serving during the COVID-19 pandemic is up significantly. Crises often create opportunities. When a hurricane strikes and thousands of people are flooded out of their homes, we send water and other supplies by the truckloads, we donate money, and some of us volunteer to go to devastated areas to help people put their lives back together. When a local family loses their home in a fire, friends and neighbors step in with donations of food, clothing, furniture, and household goods. Others set up Go Fund Me pages over the internet to garner financial support to meet the immediate needs. During the quarantines of the recent months, we often heard about children who lost a primary source of food because they were out of school and did not receive the free breakfast and lunch they were accustomed to. Churches, schools, restaurants, and food banks answered the needs by providing to-go meals for these hungry children and their families. We heard about elderly folk who could not get out to the grocery or drug store, so others who were less vulnerable volunteered to deliver groceries and prescriptions to their doorsteps. It's one of the more encouraging aspects of what we have endured for the last sixteen months.

The problem with these reactionary moments of serving is that when the large event which prompted people to get involved is over, the serving ends. Life gets busy and we forget about needs that are not publicized so much. However, needs don't go away when public interest fades.

And it is also true that serving has become popular in many other public avenues. Businesses organize opportunities for employees to "give back" by helping build a Habitat house or collecting food for a food pantry. It has become an effective marketing strategy for a business to incorporate serving into their corporate culture. This relatively new phenomenon has prompted business leaders use their companies and skills to serve instead of simply making money because . . .

- They know the best way to leave a legacy is through service.

- They know focusing on serving others is actually more profitable than focusing solely on profit.

- They change by helping people, so they desire to help others more.

- They're aware that if you live for the applause, you'll die from lack of it.

- They know it's the most fulfilling way to run a business and to live life.[4]

Additionally, schools encourage their students to be engaged in service. Some schools now require a certain number of hours serving in order to graduate. Presumably, this emphasis on serving will instill in the students the same desire to serve people in need as their ability to conjugate a sentence or solve mathematic equations or understand history. College scholarships often require service projects or a number of volunteer hours. Admissions counselors look at academic achievement as well as community involvement, especially service opportunities. Athletic teams engage in serving as a

---

4 Accessed May 15, 2021. https://addicted2success.com/entrepreneur-profile/5-reasons-why-the-best-entrepreneurs-use-their-companies-to-serve-others/

way of building camaraderie. I live in a college town where college football is king. I tell people the university football stadium is the biggest church in town. When our local team serves people in need in our community, it makes the evening news on all the local stations. People respond and join in meeting the needs when they see these local leaders, especially our young athletes, setting the example.

Currently, I believe there is more attention given to serving than any time in recent memory except perhaps during World War II when ordinary citizens were asked to do their part to help win the war. Women stepped up to fill jobs when men were drafted into the military, families planted victory gardens and every citizen was subject to rations of sugar or coffee or gasoline. There were all sorts of other ways to "help the cause" and most folks joined in the effort to serve one another. I think this sense of service is beginning to resurface, so I am hopeful. But, this does not answer our question: Why do some people serve and others do not?

For years, I have watched from the vantage point of the local church, working with thousands of individuals and churches, equipping them to serve people in need in their community. This is my assessment: First, many people have not grasped the importance of serving (for reasons I will explore in later chapters), and second, many people who sincerely want to serve think they don't have time or simply don't know where to start. Others are afraid of getting in over their heads. Still others are afraid of people they don't know and are unsure of how to deal with people in extreme need. One by one I will look at these reasons for not serving with the belief that we can move the needle of serving noticeably in the next few years.

WHY ME?

While all the reasons I've addressed for writing this book are true, they do not say it all. I have spent the last twenty-six years motivating, teaching, and organizing people to serve by seeing a need and meeting the need. My journey has led me to this point. I have written this book because I have something to say about serving. It is time to share what I have learned. For me, it's a matter of stewardship.

Stewardship is a common word, used more often in church than elsewhere. It is the idea that certain talents, skills, and experiences have been given to us for the purpose of sharing them with others. What we have been given, we are to use as good stewards of the investment that God and others have made in us. Our parents, teachers, church and community leaders instruct and encourage us to develop our talents and skills, our knowledge and understanding, our sense of empathy and compassion. I believe God has set me on this journey that has brought me to writing this book because I am passionate about serving. I pay attention when the evening news tells a story about people helping others. I buy and read every book I can find about serving. I perk up when I hear others talk about serving and I am eager to learn from their experiences. I want to see a world full of Emilys, Millards and Aubreys whose stories are told in the opening section of this chapter. I am a compassionary and I want to encourage more people to join me.

I do not expect everyone to be as passionate as I am, but I believe the world would be a better place if more people served those in need. I believe it is not only possible but also necessary to think seriously about the importance of serving and finding a place to serve. I believe our communities would be more wholesome and healthier if more people adopted an attitude of serving in everything they do. I believe every person who takes up a life of serving will find the peace and satisfaction they yearn for.

If you are someone who has not been very involved in serving but are open to learning more about it, read on. If you are a person who has experienced some of the joy that comes from serving but have difficulty getting past the distractions life puts in your way, read on. If you are a person who serves but would like to have an even deeper experience when you serve, read on. If you are a person who is troubled by the divisiveness that has come to characterize our country and want to do something about that, read on. Finally, if you are a person who enjoys serving but need help in connecting your spiritual values to your serving, by all means, read on. Want to be a compassionary? Read on!

Chapter Two

THE HIGHEST CALLING

*If you believe the teachings of Christ, every decision you
make in life should be evaluated by your ability and God's
current assignment to meet the needs of and to love and
care for others. Our desire to grow, mature and gain experience in our careers and businesses must always come
in second place to the care and serving of others. Always.*
--MARK MAXWELL

The room was pregnant with expectation. The small group of
men gathered there were mindful of the tradition they were
about to observe—an important event in their history and a
solemn occasion by itself. But on this night, they felt the pres-
sures that had been mounting around them for a while.

This night was different. Observance of their longstanding
tradition was symbolic and serious, but there was an unusual
feeling in the room and everyone knew it. Danger? Anticipation? Fear?

Things were happening on two levels, the obvious and the
hidden, spoken and unspoken, corporate and personal. As
usual, each man felt the reverence and connection with his

past that came with observing tradition. It was a good, warm feeling, and being together for this occasion made it all the better. If they observed this tradition alone, it would have been satisfying, but being together was better--like Christmas dinner when the whole family is present.

On the inside, each man was keenly aware of recent events that made this occasion even more suspenseful than usual. They had been together for a while and enjoyed a sense of community, almost like family, but there was nothing official about their group. They were not a club or clan or official body, but they were bound together by their common relationship to their leader. He was the kind of leader who often attracts followers—charismatic, wise, charming, mysterious. He attracted people everywhere he went, and this small group of men had become his inner circle. They were drawn to him as much because of his enigmatic ways as by his uncommon wisdom. They devoured every word he spoke.

But things had not gone well recently. As their leader's popularity grew, local politicians became more and more troubled. They saw where things were headed; they were convinced this man was playing to the masses, misleading gullible followers to think he could give them what they wanted—freedom and prosperity. How many times has this scenario played out in history? People feel oppressed, depressed, and distressed, longing for freedom and looking for someone to provide the way to a better, more prosperous life. These are the things all people hope for, and they are most vulnerable when a charismatic personality offers a new sense of hope. Along comes a man who promises to give them what they yearn for. They throw caution to the wind, ignoring the dangers of unfulfilled promises and before you can say, "we've heard it all before," they join together in a movement that is more emotion than reason.

Such scenarios frighten some powerful people. The politicians had been talking for some time about exposing this leader for the charlatan they believed him to be. If necessary, they were willing to take matters into their own hands and have him assassinated. It was a political gamble of the highest order. If they were right about the popular, persuasive leader (and there was absolutely no doubt in their minds about that), they were not only justified in their plans but would eventually garner the praise of a grateful citizenry. If they were wrong? Well, it could cost a man's life but what is that compared to the possibility of many lives lost? The math made their plans defensible.

All of this was coming to a head when the traditional ceremony neared. This occasion brought its own meaningful reflection even without the concerns of recent developments, and the men approached the meal with greater anticipation than normal. To say they were attentive would be a gross understatement. They were on the edge of their seats, anxious and eager to see how this important tradition would play out. This was the setting in which a remarkable, surprising event took place.

As the group settled in for the ceremony, their leader took his place just as they expected. All eyes were focused on him, all ears tuned in. The traditional meal was ready; the men were waiting for the familiar words to begin the event. Traditions are powerful things. They fill our minds with words and thoughts based on our previous experiences. That's not a bad thing; it feels comfortable, familiar, and satisfying. It was customary that the head of the family would speak before this special meal to explain its meaning, not because anyone had forgotten but because it was worth speaking aloud. In our culture, we remember the Pledge of Allegiance word for word without actually saying it, but it's not enough merely to reference the Pledge: "Let's take a moment as we remember the Pledge of Allegiance to the flag." We say it out loud and we say it together because we *need* to say it. That's how we express our allegiance to our country. That's what the men in the room were expecting—some well-chosen words from the deepest thinker they ever met about the meal they were about to partake.

But that's not what happened. In fact, their leader didn't speak at all. Instead, he began to serve his friends as he prepared them for the meal. He took a basin and a towel and he moved from his place of honor to the place of service. This was the last thing they expected—this teacher who made them think more deeply than ever before, who did such strange and wonderful things, did for them what the lowest servant in the house was supposed to do! He washed their feet.

Context is everything, the stage on which actions and words make sense. In this case, the context--expectations of the traditions of Passover, awareness of what was surely a collision course with the Jewish leaders, blindness to the ritual meal preparation (it had not occurred to a single one of the disciples to do the customary foot washing before the meal)—shined the brightest possible spotlight on Jesus' actions. What had not been done, either because everyone forgot it or, more likely, because no one else would consider doing it, Jesus did. He wrapped himself with a towel, poured water into a basin and went from disciple to disciple washing their feet. They were humbled and maybe humiliated ... for good reason.

I preached and taught on this incredibly important event in Jesus' life for many years without getting its full message. From the earliest days of the church, Jesus followers have remembered the Lord's Supper as one of the most important, memorable, holy events in his life and ministry. For more than two thousand years Christians have participated in observances of the Lord's Supper (Communion or Eucharist as some traditions call it), as a remembrance of Jesus' sacrificial death that makes forgiveness and acceptance by a perfect God possible. Without question, that is its purpose.

But what happened as part of that once-in-all-history event is a message second only to its primary meaning. **Jesus elevated serving to the highest calling a person can aspire to.** The fact that he did what he did when he did it—in the crescendo of events around him AND in the context of Passover—cannot be missed. He washed the disciples' feet not because it was important that they have clean feet nor that the tradition of foot washing was too important to be neglected, *but because it provided a simple, memorable way teach his inner circle of followers the place of serving. It is nothing less than the highest calling a person can aspire to.*

When Jesus' public ministry was drawing to a close,[5] he chose to demonstrate the priority of serving for those who would have the responsibility of telling the world about him: "I have set before you an example that you should do as I have done for you" (John 13:15). The "when" of this event is what makes serving a priority in following Jesus. At the time when

---

5 John's reporting of this event is telling: "It was just before the Passover Feast. Jesus knew that the time had come for him to leave this world and go to the Father. Having loved his own who were in the world, he now showed them the full extent of his love" (John 13:1 NIV)

every word and action of Jesus carried enormous meaning and magnitude, Jesus specifically and deliberately chose to serve his disciples by performing a duty that was considered appropriate for a slave or household servant.

Only Peter's response is reported in John 13. The impetuous, quick-to-speak-before-thinking disciple objected to Jesus washing his feet, then relented, then embraced it just as quickly. When Jesus told Peter, "If I do not wash you, you have no share with me," Peter declared, "Lord, not my feet only but also my hands and my head." Peter was all in. But not all of the disciples were so quick to accept this new example (and even Peter soon faltered as Jesus predicted later that same night). Most of them were aghast at what Jesus did; no doubt some of them were embarrassed like we are when reminded of an important detail such as starting to eat before the Blessing is said. But the disciples never forgot.

I want to adamantly affirm that the priority of serving exemplified in Jesus' washing the disciples' feet is THE message for today. Even if this event in John 13 were the only instance in which Jesus pointed out the importance of serving--and it most certainly is not as we will see in the remainder of this chapter--it would be enough to give serving a prominent place in discipleship.

> JESUS ELEVATED SERVING TO THE HIGHEST CALLING A PERSON CAN ASPIRE TO. THE FACT THAT HE DID *WHAT* HE DID *WHEN* HE DID IT—IN THE CRESCENDO OF EVENTS AROUND HIM AND IN THE CONTEXT OF PASSOVER—CANNOT BE MISSED.

I invite you to ponder the benefits of serving—what it does for us when we participate, what it does to build community, what it does to alleviate so many needs of so many people in so many places. And while you're at it, look at some other teachings and actions of Jesus. I think you'll agree that serving is the highest calling a person can aspire to.

In times past and still today, mothers and fathers dream of seeing their children do great things. Often parents or grandparents would hope that one of their sons or grandsons would become a doctor or a lawyer or, in especially pious or religious families, a preacher or priest, as if that were the highest calling a person could aspire to. When I was a teenager and began to sense God calling me to "full-time Christian service", the role of pastor/preacher was at the top of the list in terms of respect and status in my mind. That's probably why it took me about six years to begin to see myself in that role. I did not feel worthy or gifted to be a preacher. In my world, a preacher was as respectable and honorable a profession as you could choose. (Let the record show my mother never encouraged me to be a preacher.) But now, on this side of my career as a minister, I don't see the role of preacher or pastor as the most important. Now I see and fully believe that serving people in need is a higher calling.

The image of a towel-wrapped, humble Jesus stooping down to wash his students' feet turns our concept of leadership upside down. Culture says it's about power and influence; Jesus says it's about serving others even in the most humble ways. Culture says it's about wealth and status; Jesus' bowing low to wash another's feet says it's about doing for others what they need . . . no matter what it is. Servant leadership is symbolized by the towel and basin, not the throne and scepter or the executive suite and six-figure paycheck. We are never more like Jesus than when we serve people in need.

Because of the example set for us in John 13, some churches have institutionalized foot washing or mandated regular washing of feet similar to the observance of Communion. Is that what Jesus intended or did the Passover simply provide an opportunity to demonstrate humble service for the thick-headed disciples? I don't know, but the more I learn about what Jesus did and how he did it, the more I believe his plan was very calculated, or to be more intentional, God-directed. I have seen that washing another's feet can be impactful, even transformational. I am not part of a Christian tradition that practices foot washing and I don't remember it as part of any church I attended in my childhood, but I believe it is gaining in popularity especially in community oriented worship. More traditional churches are including foot washing on special occasions such as when deacons (who by definition are servants) are ordained.

The foot washing episode I remember most took place in Guatemala a few years ago. A church I once served as pastor sent some members on an annual mission trip to the Central America country. Each year they went to the same location—an end-of-the-road village within sight of an active volcano. The people were as poor as you might imagine, living in tin huts with a single electric light bulb but without running water or any of the other conveniences we take for granted. One of the visiting Tennesseans had a vision of a camp in the midst of this poverty that would serve as a "city on a hill." Every year the Tennessee church sent members to build new buildings, work with the children, provide food and other necessities, and offer medical/dental clinics.

That particular year they collected suitcases full of new shoes and gave them to children in the village until the shoes were all distributed. I was so moved by the effort that I gave my sandals to a man who had nothing more than ragged, thin flaps of leather dangling from his feet. Children lined up outside the chapel building at the camp patiently waiting for their shoes. Leaders decided the American volunteers would wash the feet of the children as part of receiving new shoes. A row of chairs was set in place and children began taking a seat in the chairs as volunteers took turns washing their feet before giving them the new shoes. It became a sacred time--not solemn as there was laughter along with some embarrassment from the children to have us "rich," white folk wash their feet, but sacred for sure.

Leaders of our mission team did not pressure any volunteer to participate in foot washing, just offered it as an opportunity to serve. Almost every volunteer quickly stepped up to do it. One man and his wife on her first mission trip out of country declined to participate. No one asked why but respected their decision. However, they made the mistake of coming to watch this special ministry. As they saw the smiles on the children's faces and heard their softly spoken gratitude, they couldn't resist getting involved. They joined the other volunteers, stooped down to wash children's feet, were overcome with emotion and tears flowed. The humble act of washing feet touched them at the deepest part of their being. Their humility and love were palpable. I believe they felt closer to God at that moment than ever before. Humbling themselves to serve others was the stage on which this transforming experience played out . . . again!

WAIT! THERE IS MORE

Have you ever wondered what the family and friends of the disciples thought about their loved ones following Jesus, walking away from their fishing nets, tax tables, and other professions to tag along behind an unproven teacher? The Gospels do not provide much information; it wasn't important when they were written. Perhaps these family members thought it was a short-term thing, maybe a week or two, but when the weeks dragged into months and months into years, they must have wondered when their husband or son or father was coming home. They must have talked about how long the men had been gone and why they left in the first place. Then, as word of the movement around Jesus gathered steam and stories of the wonderful things he was doing got back to them, they may have changed their thinking from concern to excitement. I can imagine the families bragging to their neighbors, "You know, my James is with Jesus. Jesus handpicked him!" It would not have been the first-time parents rode the coattails of their children to popularity in their own community.

Then one day, the mother of two of them—James and John—couldn't help herself. A lot of people were talking about Jesus being the long awaited Messiah, the One of whom the prophets spoke. More than a few believed he would restore Israel and they weren't bashful about saying so. So, this mother went to Jesus and asked if her boys could be given special positions of leadership in the Nazarene's movement. She wasn't willing for her ambitions to be fulfilled in the normal course of events; she needed to intervene on behalf of her sons.

When the other ten disciples got wind of her request, they were incensed. How dare she try to influence Jesus in choosing his deputies! How dare she lobby for James and John to the neglect of the others! As usual, Jesus quelled the conflict as quickly as he stilled the storm by reminding all of them, including the ambitious mother, that serving is the highest calling. He said his way is the opposite of ambition and pride. His way is serving. Success in his movement is not measured by achievement or recognition but by humble service. Then, to make sure all of them got the point, he added: "I came not to be served but to serve."

The point was crystal clear for the disciples . . . and for the mother of James and John. Her request was not just denied; it was rebuked. She may have felt ashamed and she should have. The disciples felt chastised and they should have. The lesson for us is serving is the highest calling. It's what he expects, the way he measures obedience and faithfulness.

I wish I had understood that lesson earlier in life. It's ironic that I went to seminary to learn how to be a minister and preacher. I took all the classes required to obtain the appropriate degree for my chosen profession. I spent a great deal of time studying the Bible in the original languages, and I had years of lessons on Christian theology from the ancients to the present. But I did not grasp the value, much less the priority, of serving. In fact, my seminary days were marked by the same competitive drive that is common for all serious academics. I constantly measured myself against those I perceived to be the cream of the crop, always coming up short. And that competitive drive did not wane when I took my place in the ranks of professional ministry. If anything, it intensified. So-and-so has a bigger church than I have; so-and-so has already moved up the denominational ladder. *I wish I were as good as him. I wish I could preach like him. I wish I could write like him.*

But Jesus made serving the highest calling. If I had understood that in my early days of ministry, I could have saved myself a great deal of emotional pain. More importantly, I could have been a better example for and minister to those God gave me to serve. My ministry would have had more authenticity and it would have been more effective. It should not have taken me thirty years to grasp the priority of serving . . . for all Jesus followers and especially those of us who make our living telling others about him.

Chapter Three

IT'S A SPIRITUAL THING

First, there's the job-where the goal is simply to earn a living and support your family. Then there's the career--where you trace your progress through various appointments and achievements. Finally, there's the calling-- the ideal blend of activity and character that makes work inseparable from life.
--ROBERT BELLA

I am a convert to the priority of serving. My dream is that serving will become so widespread and so highly valued that when the average person on the street is asked what it means to be a Christian, whether or not that person is a believer, the first answer will be, "A Christian is a person who serves others." Right now, that's not the answer anyone would offer. The Barna Group conducted a 2010 study into what Americans think is Christianity's contribution to society. A meager nineteen percent said Christians have "helped poor or underprivileged people have a better life." While this was the strongest answer to what Christianity has done for society, it was a very low score. Even more, twenty-five percent, one in four, said they could not "think of a single positive contribution made by Christians in recent years"![6] Unfortunately, my goal is still a dream.

If I were writing a book on spiritual disciplines, Chapter One would be about serving others. Okay, I am biased, but I can support my conviction from the life and teachings of Jesus—his sermon at Nazareth when he read from Isaiah that he came to help people in need (Lk. 4), the incident in which James' and John's mother asked that they be given places of status when Jesus established his kingdom and she was told Jesus came not to be served but to serve (Mt. 20), the parable of the Good Samaritan (Lk. 10), his statement about how we can serve him (Mt. 25), and his washing of the disciples' feet (Jn. 13). All of these examples are part of my belief that serving is the highest calling a person can aspire to.

MORE THAN A VOCATION

I am using the word *calling* deliberately. It suggests more than a vocation which may only be employment that enables us to pay the bills. Most of us have a job. We are employed by a company or organization that pays us in exchange for our work. This is a good arrangement and a necessary one for most of us.

A calling is "fuzzier" but more fulfilling. A calling comes from some-

> A CALLING COMES FROM SOMEWHERE INSIDE US. IT MAY OR MAY NOT HAVE ANYTHING TO DO WITH A JOB. IT'S A SPIRITUAL THING.

---

6 www.barna.com/research/americans-say-serving-the-needy-is-christianitys-biggest-contribution-to-society/ October 25, 2010, accessed April 4, 2021.

where inside us. It may or may not have anything to do with a job. It's a spiritual thing. I believe it comes from God. It's what we were made for. It's the niche we fit like no other. It's our purpose. When we act according to our calling, we feel a deeper sense of satisfaction than a paycheck can provide.

How many times have you done something that produced deep feelings of joy and satisfaction and wondered why you can't have those feelings in your job? The reason may be that your job and your calling are not well matched. Blessed is the person for whom their job and their calling are one and the same. A calling is an awareness of and commitment to a compelling sense of purpose. People of faith believe their calling comes from God and that it can be for anything—a nurse who feels called to care for the sick, a teacher who feels called to help students learn what they need to thrive, a policeman who feels called to keep his community safe, a businessperson who feels called to provide fulfilling work for his employees and services for the community, a farmer who feels called to produce food to feed others.

Calling and purpose are almost synonymous. Both are an inner sense of who you are and why you're here. I make a distinction between the two in this way: A purpose is a vital sense of giftedness or responsibility to do a certain thing with your life; a calling is the same but with the added sense that this giftedness or responsibility comes from God. Your calling has a spiritual dimension and usually relates to your gifts, but not necessarily. If you have a gift for helping others learn, that may indicate your calling to be a teacher. On the other hand, you may have a gift to help children learn and you may be very good at it, but you may feel you are called to serve elderly people who are lonely. In this case, your calling and your gift are different. If you have a knack for designing machines, that may indicate your giftedness to be an engineer. On the other hand, you may have the ability to be a good engineer but have a calling to serve disadvantaged children.

See the difference? I do not intend to de-value *purpose* as a useful way to finding meaning for one's life. It's vitally important, but please hear me: Everyone has a purpose, even those who do not outwardly or obviously appear to have anything to offer, for example, persons with overwhelming needs such as children who have debilitating disabilities or those who are economically disadvantaged and totally powerless. Perhaps their purpose is to provide the rest of us an opportunity to serve.

I believe everyone has a calling—a purpose from God—whether or not they believe in God. And I believe that calling *always* involves serving others. The Bible documents God's compassion for the poor and marginalized as one of his essential characteristics, so it stands to reason that God's calling on each person would involve serving others. Is it too much to say serving is part of what God meant when he told Adam and Eve they were to take care of the earth and have dominion over it? Look again at the ministry of Jesus and the examples we've already cited. If Jesus came to show us what God is like, then his example not only demonstrated the compassion of the Father but also his expectation of his people. I will say it again: our calling always involves serving others. See Tom's story at the end of this chapter.

Here is the thing. We **yearn** to make a difference and know that we are living out our purpose. Sadly, jobs seldom provide that. My good friend Bill shared his frustration with his job in conversation with me and it wasn't the first time. He said he just wanted to be appreciated for what he does, he wants to know that he has made a difference, that he will be missed when he's gone. When he gets to heaven, Bill would like to be able to look around and see at least one person who says he is there because of him. Bill represents many, many people who languish in unfulfilling jobs that do not match their calling.

This is the beauty of Jesus' call to serve others. Anyone can do it. It doesn't require special talents or skills. It does require compassion, humility and courage (more about these in Chapter 7), but the fact is anyone can serve others. In his usually insightful way, Martin Luther King, Jr. said, "Everyone can be great because everyone can serve. You don't have to have a college degree to serve. You don't even have to make your subject and verb agree to serve. You only need a heart full of grace. A soul generated by love."

Perhaps you've gotten the impression that a calling to serve is totally different from your occupation, that the two are not related, if not mutually exclusive. Not so. In fact, some people are discovering the place of serving within their occupation. Their place of employment is the stage on which their serving takes place. In *Dare to Serve: How to Drive Superior Results by Serving Others*,[7] Cheryl Bachelder outlines her plan to make service the strategy for business. As the CEO of Popeye's Louisiana Kitchen, Inc., she has led her company in a remarkable turnaround from one of the poorest performing fast-food restaurant chains in the country to one of the best in a relatively short time. She attributes the turnaround to the

---

7 Cheryl Bachelder. *Dare to Serve: How to Drive Superior Results by Serving Others*. Oakland, CA: Berrett-Koehler Puiblishers, 2015.

implementation of serving others—customers, franchisees, vendors, employees—as their new way of doing business. .

Another example is attorney Mark Maxwell who specializes is legal matters pertaining to the music business. His book *Networking Kills: Success Through Serving* makes a compelling case against the popular success strategy of networking in favor of serving others as a better way to achieve the kind of success most people want. He says networking is disingenuous and self-serving; serving is genuine and others oriented. He says networking kills creativity, authentic relationships, life, and love. "The problem with networking," says Maxwell, "is that no matter how you slice it or dress it up (win/win, generosity to others, palms down, etc.), the root or foundation of networking is based on exploitation and selfishness, on taking from others and using others for your own benefit. And there is something deep inside of all of us (I call it the image of God), that fights against that selfish pathway to success."[8]

Serving is Mark Maxwell's way of practicing law. He does the same work as any other attorney—creating legal documents that protect the interests of his clients, advising his clients as to the strictures of the law regarding the issues they bring to him—but he sees himself as serving them. He is genuinely interested in meeting their needs beyond the best practices of law. As a result, he cultivates and enjoys relationships with his clients, and they trust him more deeply.

Maxwell is also an adjunct professor at Belmont University in Nashville focusing on the legal aspect of the music business.

---

8 Maxwell, Mark, *Networking Kills: Success Through Serving* (Desolation Row Press, Nashville, 2015), pp. 60-61.

He has taken the same approach to teaching. He sees himself as serving the students more than teaching them:

> Each week, I try to efficiently nail my law practice responsibilities so I can spend extra time on the campus. Though not required for any course, I strongly encourage each one of my students to meet with me outside of class at least once that semester, usually for coffee at Bongo Java where my vision for Belmont began. A large number of students do take me up on it, and for many, that is the start of a series of meetings we will have throughout their college days and afterward…. I listen to them intently, learn their stories, and pray in those sacred moments for less of my opinions and guesses and more of the words of God to flow through me.[9]

A STORY OF SERVING

My friend Wayne Smith has been on a journey for several years as a result of his sense of call to serve people in need. First as a school principal, Wayne saw himself not as an administrator or even a leader but as one serving the students, teachers, and staff at his school. Wayne feels he was called by God to serve in that role and believes his work was more effective because of his perspective as a servant. As his career was ending, Wayne was tapped by his church leaders to be part of a group to educate the congregation about HIV and AIDS. He volunteered to serve HIV patients in a local hospital and it took courage to push past the rampant misinformation about HIV. This was before a successful treatment was in place when false assumptions about the spread of the disease caused great

---

9 Maxwell, p. 123.

fear and prejudice toward those who were HIV positive. In spite of the driving fears and uncaring attitudes he encountered, Wayne found that the patients he met were simply people who were sick. Because of their particular disease, they were isolated and ostracized. Wayne's heart went out to these twenty-first century "lepers".

At dinner with friends, the subject of Wayne's pending retirement came up. One friend asked what he planned to do in retirement and he answered, "I don't have any plans right now." She rephrased her question, "If you had the desire of your heart, what would you do?" Wayne answered promptly, "I would do HIV ministry." Even he was a little surprised by his response. He'd felt drawn to victims of HIV, but he'd never verbalized a desire to serve them. When he retired from the school system in 2001, he became more involved in caring for people with HIV. Many of them needed help navigating the labyrinth of health and social services systems. Wayne stepped in. He referred them to the appropriate resources. He drove them to appointments. He assisted in getting help with utilities and rent. Slowly, over the years Wayne developed a ministry to people with HIV based out of his church. There was never a proposal or formal decision by the church to begin this ministry. It just evolved over time.

Today, Samaritan Ministry serves about 150 clients. Each person receives a small grocery delivery monthly, invitations to two large social events a year at the church, and numerous benevolent services from Wayne Smith. In some cases, these people do not have family to help them either because their family has withdrawn from them or because they have withdrawn from their family. Wayne is family for them. And when they die, Wayne takes care of the arrangements and sometimes even serves as the minister at their funeral.

Wayne does what he does as a result of a calling to serve that was revealed to him slowly over time.[10] His attitude of serving which began in his early career shifted from the school environment to a medical and social environment. The catalyst in his calling was his compassion for needs of HIV-infected people who were sick, lonely, and hurting due to the stigma of AIDS. He did not seek this role. He did not expect it and was initially surprised by his own passion to serve this community. I have seen firsthand the special relationship Wayne has with his clients, or friends as he prefers to call them. They know he loves them, they know he will help them, and they trust him more than they trust any other person in this world. No one who knows Wayne and his ministry questions whether this is his calling.

---

10 Wayne Smith's story comes from personal conversation with the author, March, 2021.

SUCCESS THROUGH SERVING

Ask most people what makes for a successful life, and they will say something like "a good job with good pay and good standing in the community." By this standard, Tom Steele was successful. For a long time, he lived the American dream. He owned his own businesses—five of them, to be exact—and enjoyed no small prestige in his community. He was a leader in his church including running several successful capital campaigns. He was tagged to lead the community United Way annual campaign, served as President of the Chamber of Commerce, and had other community leadership roles. He was well respected and trusted. He had worked hard to reach his goals and anyone who knew Tom was convinced he'd accomplished them. Yet, he was nagged with the question: "When is it enough?"

Over a period of time and self-reflection, Tom thought about what he wanted out of life and he had to admit something was missing. There was a void he couldn't describe but he knew it was there. So, in his late fifties, Tom decided to sell his businesses—all of them—and his home, and take a different, more relaxed approach to life. He bought a houseboat and began making long trips up and down the waterways of the Eastern U.S. He thrived on the change of pace and felt the stress of having so many responsibilities subside. Life was good.

After a few years of the easy life, Tom needed a new challenge. One day when he was reading the morning newspaper, he scanned the classified ads and one of them jumped off the page. It was an ad for a volunteer coordinator at a local non-profit that ministers to the homeless. Tom says the ad was like a bright light. He wasn't looking for a job, but this ad so captivated him that he called that day to apply for the position. At one time he had as many as 150 employees under his supervision, so he felt he could handle the job of working with a couple of dozen volunteers. He got the job and worked there for more than eight years.

After his successful business career and his more leisurely travels, Tom recalls this as one of the happiest times of his life. He was surprised at how much he enjoyed serving the homeless and spending time with them. He did his job of co-ordinating the volunteers at the agency, but he saw his real job as helping their homeless clients.

He distinctly remembers a day when he felt so happy to be doing what he was doing that he almost skipped down the street on his way to lunch at the café he went to every day. Making money and enjoying a sterling reputation in his com-munity had not made him as happy as serving people from the street. They were powerless but unpretentious, dirty and aimless but sincere and, for the most part, honest, constantly in need of help but resilient and real to the core. Tom loved them. Furthermore, they loved him.

The agency observed the usual holidays when they were closed and no services were offered. Because he enjoyed being with the people so much, Tom would buy several dozen Krispy Kreme donuts to take them to the office, put on a pot of coffee and sit around with the people talking and enjoying one another's company like neighbors sitting on his front porch for the morning.

Looking back, Tom says it was when he "worked" at the homeless agency that he found his purpose in life. He is convinced God put him there. His purpose is to love people in need, to respect them and serve their needs as best he can. It is to allow God to use him as a channel of mercy and grace for people who need it because the world has no place for them. His purpose is to put God's love into simple actions and occasional words. In the process of serving others, Tom discovered that God's love, which he thought he understood, is deeper and wider than he ever imagined.

Tom is still living out his purpose, serving people in need. Now in his seventies, he volunteers twice a week in a community program that provides food, assistance with utilities, and other forms of help for people who cannot provide for themselves. It's still time with the people that he enjoys the most. The "work" may be slightly different, but the "rewards" are the same. Tom is a happy compassionary.

PART TWO

Chapter Four

HAPPINESS TRIFECTA

*Those who are happiest are those
who do the most for others.*
--Booker T. Washington

If you've ever tried to recruit volunteers to serve people in
need, there's a good chance your "sales pitch" included something like, "You'll feel good when you do it!" You said that
because it's true. We do in fact feel good when we serve. As a
pastor, I often told my congregation there is a special joy that
comes from serving. Most people agreed and remembered
that part of their serving experience. A minister friend told
that to her sister-in-law, a non-churched volunteer, whose two
siblings and their spouses were all involved in ministry. After
a few months of volunteering in her community, she told her
family how deeply she was affected by the hours of serving
she had been doing and offered to volunteer in each sibling's
preferred ministry over the next year. For the first time, she
understood their call to serve others and she was happier than
she had been in many years.

Why? Why do we feel good when we participate in service to others? Is it because we know it's the right thing to do, what I call "the Wilfred Brimley effect" (from his Quaker Oats commercials—"It's the right thing to do")? Is it because we believe our standing with our peers is enhanced? Is it a yearning for that inner feeling of satisfaction that we can't quite describe but know it when we feel it?

A Chinese proverb says, "If you want happiness for an hour, take a nap. If you want happiness for a day, go fishing. If you want happiness for a year, inherit a fortune. If you want happiness for a lifetime, help somebody."[11] This truth is echoed by any number of other wise thinkers:

"In the same degree as you are helpful, you will be happy."[12]

"Since you get more joy out of giving joy to others, you should put a good deal of thought into the happiness that you are able to give."[13]

"Those who are the happiest are those who do the most for others."[14]

"Happiness is a by-product of an effort to make someone else happy."[15]

---

11 Jenny Santi, "The Secret to Happiness is Helping Others." https://time.com/collection/guide-to-happiness/4070299/secret-to-happiness/ accessed May 17, 2021

12 Karl Reiland, https://www.energizeinc.com/directory/volunteerism-quotes/helping, accessed May 23, 2021.

13 Eleanor Roosevelt, https://www.motivationalwellbeing.com/55-meaningful-quotes-about-helping-others.html, accessed May 23, 2021.

14 Booker T. Washington, https://www.motivationalwellbeing.com/55-meaningful-quotes-about-helping-others.html, accessed May 23, 2021.

15 Gretta Brooker Palmer, https://www.motivationalwellbeing.com/55-meaningful-quotes-about-helping-others.html, accessed May 23, 2021.

I believe that serving people in need promises happiness three times over. This Happiness Trifecta occurs because we are hard-wired to serve, because it connects us more closely with others, and because it gives us purpose and meaning. Let's focus on each of these happiness effects in hopes of not only enhancing your understanding of what happens inside us when we serve, but also confirming your conviction to serve as much as you can.

HARD-WIRED TO SERVE

You may have heard of the "helper's high." This is a warm, good feeling that comes whenever we serve people in need, akin to a "runner's high" that comes when a runner finishes a good run. This "high" is the release of endorphins in the brain that makes a person feel satisfied, energized, and happy.

Carolyn Schwartz, a research professor at the University of Massachusetts Medical School, examined the benefits multiple sclerosis patients experienced when they received encouraging calls from peers. She found that the patients felt significant improvement, but she also found that those making the calls had dramatic improvements to the quality of their lives.[16] So Schwartz dug deeper. She looked at more than two thousand mostly healthy Presbyterian churchgoers across the nation. She found that those who helped others were significantly happier and less depressed than those who didn't.

Neuroscience has demonstrated that serving others triggers stimuli to our brain in many positive ways. Serving actually releases oxytocin, serotonin and dopamine, hormones

---

16 https://thinklivebepositive.wordpress.com/2018/01/22/do-good-feel-good/, accessed May 23, 2021.

which have the effect of boosting our mood and counteracting the effect of cortisol, the stress hormone. Scientific studies that confirm and reconfirm the positive, biochemical responses that are hard-wired into our brain are too numerous to mention. Physicians, researchers, and patients sensed this effect for a long time without fully understanding it but now they have concrete evidence to explain these results.

SERVING REDUCES MORTALITY BY 22 PERCENT TO 44 PERCENT. PEOPLE WHO VOLUNTEER HAVE 29 PERCENT LOWER RISK OF HIGH BLOOD PRESSURE, 17 PERCENT LOWER RISK OF INFLAMMATION LEVELS, AND SPEND 38 PERCENT FEWER NIGHTS IN THE HOSPITAL.

Another contribution to this line of research comes at the issue from a different direction. Marta Zaraska has examined what makes some people live longer than others and, interestingly, debunks conventional thinking that says diet and exercise are the keys to longevity. Her book *Growing Young: How Friendship, Kindness, and Optimism Can Help You Live to 100* makes cogent arguments for the longevity benefits of serving others alongside other positive traits. After years of research, Zaraska concludes that "diet and exercise [are] not the most important things . . . to encourage my family's longevity. Instead of shopping for organic goji berries, I should concentrate on our social lives and [emotional] makeup. I should look for a purpose in life, not the best fitness tracker."[17]

17 Marta Zaraska, *Growing Young: How Friendship, Kindness and Optimism Can Help You To Live To 100*. Random House: Canada, 2020, p. 15.

Zaraska agrees with many other scientists who have studied the benefits of serving when she says we have a caregiving system built within us. This system is composed of biological-chemical processes in our brain that encourage us to care for others. There are two aspects to this caregiving system—one is reward-inducing and the other is stress-reducing. She supports her conclusions with these stats:

- serving reduces mortality by 22 percent to 44 percent,

- people who volunteer have 29 percent lower risk of high blood pressure,

- volunteers experience 17 percent lower risk of inflammation levels,

- those who serve spend 38 percent fewer nights in the hospital.[18]

By any standard, these statistics are impressive.

One of the most fascinating parts of what Zaraska says about the happiness and longevity benefits to serving others is her own personal (admittedly unscientific) experiment to see if serving others does in fact enhance our mood. Over seven days she alternated between going about her normal activities on some days and focusing on showing others kindness on other days. For example, on one of her "kindness days," she left a smiley face sticky note on a neighbor's car. She bought and delivered chocolates for a woman at the library. In the evening, she left five-star ratings for her favorite restaurants. "I don't know whether my telomeres got longer and whether my cortisol response healthier, but I certainly felt better, happier. Broccoli

---

18 Zaraska, p. 193.

has never given me this feeling, that's for sure," she concludes.[19] Imagine how she would have felt if in addition to sticky notes and five-star restaurant ratings, Zaraska had mentored a lonely, troubled teenager or helped a newcomer learn English as a second language.

As impressive as Marta Zaraska's book and others' work on the emotional benefits of serving are, I can't leave this first effect of the Happiness Trifecta without offering my own conclusion: God made us to serve others. If we are hard-wired to serve, is it not because God made us that way? Medical science was a long time in discovering the cause of heart attacks, yet the biological reasons were there all along. God put the human body together in such a way that too many plaque-producing foods may lead to heart disease and death. In the same way, we now know that serving boosts your mood and well-being because of hormones that are part of our physical makeup. These are the facts, and compelling facts they are. Serving others makes us happy. A "helper's high" is better than pills, better than ice cream, better than ten consecutive positive days on the stock market. A proven way to a better life is found in serving people in need.

SERVING STRENGTHENS OUR CONNECTIONS WITH OTHERS

The second part of the Happiness Trifecta is that serving strengthens our connections with others.[20] Some serving is done

---

19 Zaraska, p. 204.

20 One of the benefits of an Inasmuch Day is people in the church become acquainted with others in the church they did not know prior to the event. Most church folk hang with the same few friends in their church. They may see others in the church and are friendly with them, but they do not know them because they don't spend time with them. If they serve on the same team in an Inasmuch Day, they get to know each other by building memories together.

alone—making stuffed animals for police officers to give children caught in circumstances of domestic violence or cooking a meal for a neighbor recovering from surgery. But most of the time, we serve with and for others—staffing a non-profit that serves the homeless, delivering for Meals on Wheels to the elderly, building a wheelchair ramp with a construction team for a disabled veteran. Serving strengthens your connections with others by spending time with coworkers.

Do you really need convincing that meaningful relationships are beneficial? We were created as social beings. We need other people. From the beginning of creation, God saw that it was not good for Adam to be alone and he created a partner for him. We need interaction with others, some of us (extroverts) more than others (introverts), but we **all** need relationships. Anything that helps us engage with other people, especially if it involves a mutual interest, meets one of our basic human needs.[21] Consider this from Marta Zaraska, "If you can do just one thing for your health and longevity, that thing should be finding a great partner and committing to the relationship. . . . And then there is friendship—the close second when it comes to boosting your centenarian potential."[22]

Companions in service are important, but the most significant connections you will make are with those you serve. Getting to know each person in need and learning about each unique situation provides an opportunity to understand the

---

21 One of the benefits of an Inasmuch Day has been the quieting of church conflict. One church that was in major conflict over the dismissal of a senior pastor conducted an Inasmuch Day. The leader of the event said: "At least for one day we forgot our fighting and focused on serving people in need in our community."

22 Zaraska, p. 167.

"whys" of these needs. With that understanding, you may feel led to go "upstream," to do what you can to fix the system or to modify the circumstances that create perpetual need.

Spending time with people gives authenticity to service. People in need are accustomed to "hit-and-run" serving where a well-meaning volunteer swoops in to offer a meal or a hand or something to meet an immediate need. When there is no attempt to engage with those in need, these recipients feel as though they are simply a "target" for do-gooders, an item to be checked off the "server's" to-do list. That kind of serving may do more harm than good.

It occurred to me a few years ago that people who receive our help are doing us a favor by letting us serve them. So, I began thanking them for allowing me to serve and I have encouraged others to do the same. If even half of the bene-fits of serving are true, then people in need do us a favor by receiving our help. Just as it takes two to tango, it takes two to serve—one serving, and one being served. And if most of the benefits of serving accrue to the one serving, then those being served deserve your gratitude for letting it happen.

SERVING ENHANCES OUR SENSE OF PURPOSE

In the words of the great cinematic philosopher, Goldie Hawn, "Giving back is as good for you as it is for those you are helping because giving gives you purpose. When you have a purpose-driven life, you're a happier person."[23]

Purpose is your reason for being. It is one of the things for which you believe you were born, the cause or job or func-

------

23 Santi

EVERYONE WANTS TO THINK HE IS OF VALUE TO OTHERS. HE MATTERS. SERVING PEOPLE IN NEED GIVES YOU PURPOSE. IT NOURISHES YOUR SELF-ESTEEM IN HEALTHY WAYS. IT GIVES YOU VALUE.

tion that fits you best. It is the culmination of most of your life experiences, a sort of a destination. Happiness and purpose are not the same, but they are connected. They feed off each other. When you have a clearly defined sense of purpose, you are more satisfied and happier. When you experience happiness from living out your purpose, that purpose becomes even stronger.

Purpose is also linked to self-esteem, your sense of value. As you live out your sense of purpose, and you may have several relating to various aspects of your life, you feel appreciated and worthy. You feel you make a difference. Everyone wants to think he is of value to others, that his life matters. Serving people in need gives you purpose. It nourishes your self-esteem in healthy ways. It gives you value. I have talked with thousands of people engaged in serving and have yet to hear one person say serving does not enhance their own sense of value.

A loss of purpose is common among senior adults. Aging friends often express the same sentiment--"I don't know why I'm still here,"--which is part lament and part a wish not to linger too long in a state of complete dependence. When mental or physical health, or both, deteriorate to the point that they can no longer care for themselves, it plunges them into an especially deep feeling of grief. The seniors who are most satisfied with their later years are those who continue to find purpose, perhaps in providing genealogical information for their families or creating a sense of community to newcomers in an assisted living facility or offering wisdom gained by years of experience to a novice in their previous career. Staying mentally and physically active are important but finding purpose makes life more meaningful.

Serving people in need can give you purpose, a sense of importance and meaning because it extends your care beyond yourself. One of the most compelling confirmations of this fact is *Once a Warrior: How One Veteran Found a New Mission Closer to Home* by Jake Wood. Wood has written of his harrowing experiences as a Marine in Iraq and Afghanistan and the struggle to re-assimilate into civilian life. Even in his own difficult situation, he was so moved by devastation of the Haiti earthquake a few years ago that that he called a few Marine buddies and organized a disaster relief team to help the poor, traumatized people of Haiti. When another disaster occurred, Jake Wood did it again and again and again, eventually establishing Team Rubicon, a disaster relief organization composed primarily of veterans who know how to get things done when the need is too big for others to handle. Jake Wood received the Pat Tillman Award for Service at the 2006 ESPYs and Team Rubicon has been recognized by state and federal agencies for their superior disaster relief work.

I was drawn to the story of Jake Wood's Team Rubicon because their serving offered a new sense of purpose for veterans who found it hard to transition from the clear, crucial missions they had in war to civilian life. Instead of camaraderie and brotherhood they had experienced as soldiers, civilian life was characterized more by an attitude of what's-in-it-for-me.

Serving others provided companionship, purpose, and the satisfaction of making a difference in someone else's life. One of the crucial events that propelled Wood further into the idea of an ongoing disaster relief venture was the suicide of his Marine buddy Clay Hunt. Clay struggled more than most to find his place after war. One night when Clay came to Jake just to talk, Jake asked his friend when he felt happy. "'I'll tell you what it is," Clay said. "It's purpose. That's all it is, Jake. When I'm doing TR stuff, I have purpose, just like in the Marines. When I look in the mirror, I'm proud of the person looking back at me."[24] Clay Hunt made the same discovery others have been making for a very long time--serving others gives us deep, satisfying purpose.

SERVING MAKES GOD HAPPIER

Let me speak now to the person of faith. Yes, serving makes you happier, connects you with other people, and gives you a sense of purpose, but that's not all there is to it. When you serve, you implement God's plan to care for those who cannot care for themselves. That God has a special place in his heart for the poor and oppressed is well documented in Scripture:

> "For there will never cease to be poor in the land. Therefore, I command you, 'You shall open wide your hand to your brother, to the needy and to the poor, in your land.'" Deuteronomy 15:11

> "Feed the hungry and help those in trouble. Then your light will shine out from the darkness, and the darkness around you will be as bright as noon." Isaiah 58:10

---

24 Jake Wood, *Once a Warrior: How One Veteran Found a Mission Closer to Home.* New York: Sentinel Press, 2020, p. 131.

"Each of you should use whatever gift you have received to serve others, as faithful stewards of God's grace in its various forms." 1 Peter 4:10

"Inasmuch as you have [fed the hungry, clothed the naked, visited the imprisoned for] the least of these, my brethren, you have done it to me." Matthew 25:40

"Suppose a brother or sister is without clothes and daily food. If one of you says to him, 'Go, I wish you well; keep warm and well fed.' But does nothing about his physical needs, what good is it? . . . faith by itself, if it is not accompanied by action, is dead." James 2:15-17

All of the positive results of serving apply to the believer, but he has an additional motive for serving—fulfilling God's command to serve people in need. There is a spiritual dimension of happiness that comes to a believer when he serves. Believers have an additional reason to serve beyond meeting physical or emotional needs. They serve to share God's love. Serving others not only communicates our own care for those in need but also God's deep and abiding love and care for each man, woman, or child.

Consider this example from Sumter, South Carolina where Roosevelt has lived all his life. He worked as a janitor in the county schools and, therefore, lived meagerly all his life, but he was happy with his garden and chickens. Long after he stopped working, he lost running water in his trailer for three years and did not have the means to repair it. He did the best he could without much hope of his situation getting any better. His trailer lacked underpinning and was so cold inside at times that Roosevelt had to stay close to the open oven to stay warm. He said he had decided to give up and set about writing his obituary assuming no help was coming.

A local church learned of his plight and sent a team of volunteers to repair his plumbing and make other much-needed repairs to Roosevelt's trailer. One of the volunteers was Joel Singletary. Joel was moved by Roosevelt's contentment amidst poverty and quickly forged a deep friendship with him. Joel became Roosevelt's principle means of transportation to necessary appointments and a recipient of Roosevelt's gardening. As a way of showing his gratitude for what the church did for him, Roosevelt would fill Joel's trunk with fresh vegetables from his garden and take them to the church to give those who came by.

Roosevelt's assessment of how his life was improved is reported in a video about this story (operationinasmuch.org/stories-of-compassion/Roosevelts-story/). He says, "Joel and a whole group of his friends came and turned my life around. I appreciate it. The Lord sent them to me and it went on from there. I thank the Lord and I thank Joel."

Chapter Five

SERVING GIVES HOPE

*Do all the good you can, by all the means you can, in all
the ways you can, in all the places you can, at all the times
you can, to all the people you can, as long as you ever can.*
--JOHN WESLEY

Serving is powerful and transformative and its impact can be surprisingly wonderful. Here's one example.

Multiple churches from across the city mobilized their members in a community service project to reach the poor, disadvantaged, and marginalized. Leaders targeted a neighborhood with an especially bad reputation—high crime, drugs, poverty, illiteracy—the sort of neighborhood that the local Chamber of Commerce did not feature in its promotional materials. One leader responsible for identifying homes needing repairs went into the neighborhood, against the advice of others, and began knocking on doors. She asked residents if volunteers could provide a new roof or repair a sagging front porch or paint a house. Some of the residents declined her offer because the city and county had promised help before but never followed through. Residents were understandably skeptical and some actually turned down the chance to have their homes repaired . . . for free! However, enough residents agreed and about a dozen projects were planned for that neighborhood on the day of the event.

The survey and enlistment were several weeks prior to the Saturday workday, so some of the residents forgot about it; others had an "I'll-believe-it-when-I-see-it" attitude. Even when delivery trucks from local building supply businesses began to drop off materials for the Saturday workday, some residents still refused to believe it was real. When volunteers flooded the neighborhood on Saturday, about twenty-five teams in all, residents were incredulous but thrilled. When the sun set that day, the neighborhood looked better than it had in years. Better yet, the residents felt better than they had in years.

One week later, a team from the local community college came to the neighborhood, as they regularly did, to teach people to read and write. The illiteracy rate was high which exacerbated the poverty and poor life choices pervasive in the community. But, on this particular day, *four times as many people came to learn how to read and write as had ever come before.* Volunteers from the community college attributed the stronger turnout to the community service project the week before. Finally, someone had offered help, showed up to do the work, and completed the jobs they promised to do. They helped when no one else would.

Here's what I believe happened: When their needs were met, these residents began to have hope. *People with hope do things to help themselves.*

PAIN IS INEVITABLE; SUFFERING IS OPTIONAL.

Pain is an unavoidable part of life, pure and simple. There is no bubble of protection, no cocoon of safety from pain of some kind. When a person endures pain long enough with no relief in sight, hope can become a corresponding casualty.

It's natural for a person in pain to question whether anyone knows or cares. It is one thing to be in pain; it is something else to be in pain and believe that no one cares about you. This pain on top of pain is the very definition of suffering, but pain need not lead to suffering. If a caring person steps in to meet a sufferer's need, even if it is not possible to alleviate the pain completely, the need may not lead to suffering. Suffering comes from both the attitude of the person in pain and the fact that no one is responding to his need.

Here's an example from my volunteer work. A woman asked for help with her utility bill. Her income and expenses were very low, but she was disabled with no prospect of additional income beyond her monthly disability check. Every month her expenses exceed her income. She is on oxygen so it is critical that her power remain on. When she called us, she was beginning to feel desperate. After verifying her information, I was able to tell her that our organization would pay her entire power bill including the past due amount. This was more than she expected, and her voice trembled as she thanked me. Here's the thing: this woman did not merely receive the gift of keeping electricity flowing in her small apartment, but she also received the huge gift of hope because someone cared enough to help her. Serving does that.

Hopelessness is a dark place emotionally. All of us experience pain, but some people endure pain long enough for it to cause despair—a deep sense that the road back to normalcy is longer than we thought it would be. Perhaps some of us felt real despair for the first time in the summer of 2020 when the COVID-19 pandemic was raging, and a vaccine seemed so very far away. But we were not hopeless. We believed eventually a vaccine would be discovered and sufficient amounts would be available to protect us so that life would one day return to normal.

Hopelessness is the absence of any hope, an inability even to imagine a time when help will come, when normal life will return, when pain will end. "Take from a man his wealth, and you hinder him; take from him his purpose, and you slow him down. But take from man his hope, and you stop him. He can go on without wealth, and even without purpose, for a while. But he will not go on without hope."[25]

> HOPE IS A STOWAWAY THAT TRAVELS WITH SERVING. IT MAY NOT BE CONCEIVED OR EVEN IMAGINED, BUT IT'S THERE WORKING IN CONCERT WITH CARING DOING ITS THERAPEUTIC PART.

THE POWER OF HOPE

Psychologist Dale Archer has worked with people who suffer great loss and who have good reason to wonder if life will go on for them. "I had the privilege of working with the victims of both Hurricanes Katrina and Rita. I quickly found that there were two types of physical survivors: psychological

---

25 Brian's Lines: The Pastor's Helper. Richardson, TS: From the Ministry of Brian L. Harbour. January/February, 2002, p. 2.

victims and psychological survivors. I realized that the mindset had nothing to do with money, education, how much was lost, or how many loved ones died."[26] The difference between the victim mindset and the survivor mindset was hope. Those with a victim mindset are all consumed by their loss, refusing to help themselves. The survivors grieve, which is healthy, but they continue to persevere and fight. Archer adds a powerful statement: "Hope is often the only thing between man and the abyss. As long as a patient, individual or victim has hope, they can recover from anything and everything."[27]

SERVING DISPENSES HOPE

Hope is a stowaway that travels with serving. It may not be recognized or even imagined, but it's there working in concert with serving, doing its therapeutic part. And here's the bonus—hope lasts longer and offers to produce additional positive results. When I have the opportunity to encourage folk to serve people in need, I link help and hope together. As we serve others, we have the power to give people help and hope. Help is relief for the immediate need—food for the hungry, shelter for the homeless, an embrace for the lonely—but hope goes beyond the immediate need into the future. Hope inspires us to do what we can to help ourselves. It gives us the strength to persevere even in the direst circumstances.

No one explains this better than Helen Keller, that brilliant sufferer alone in the emptiness of blindness and deafness, a plight that might have led anyone else into madness

---

26 Dale Archer, M.D. psychologytoday.com/us/blog/reading-between-the-headlines/201307/the-power-hope, accessed May 27, 2021.

27 Archer.

and hopelessness. She writes of the time when she first met Anne Sullivan who taught her to communicate despite her severe handicaps: "Have you ever been at sea in a dense fog, when it seemed as if a tangible white darkness shut in, and the great ship, tense and anxious, groped her way toward the shore with plummet and sounding-line, and you waited with beating heart for something to happen? I was like that ship before my education began, only I was without compass or sounding line, and had no way of knowing how near the harbor was. 'Light! Give me light!' was the wordless cry of my soul, and the light of love shone on me in that very hour. I felt approaching footsteps. I stretched out my hand as I supposed it to be my mother. Someone took it, and I was caught up and held close in the arms of her who had come to reveal all things to me, and, more than all things else, to love me."[28]

Hopelessness is misery and desperation, a sense of anguish and sorrow that sometimes leads to a feeling of worthlessness. When you have no hope and no one to turn to, it's a slippery slope into feelings of emptiness and abandonment. Disappointment is a common companion, and you feel like your life has little value. These two—hopelessness and worthlessness—are often the first feelings that begin to fade when someone steps up to care and serve the needs of a hurting person.

Something like that is what happened in a North Carolina neighborhood. A day of community service focused on homes on the verge of being condemned as unlivable. One resident had no running water because his plumbing was

---

28 Helen Keller. *The Story of My Life*. Bantam Books: New York, NY, 1990, pp. 14-15.

YOU HAVE THE ABILITY TO GIVE HOPE TO PEOPLE IN NEED. BY DOING WHAT YOU CAN TO SERVE THEM AT THE POINT OF THEIR NEED, YOU HELP THEM SEE THEIR FUTURE IN A MORE POSITIVE, PROMISING WAY. non-functional, and he washed dishes with a water hose. His kitchen floor was rotted and he cooked his meals on a grill outside regardless of the weather. He was unable to do repairs himself and he couldn't afford to pay someone else to do it, so he suffered in poverty alone and silent. Like many others, he felt abandoned and worthless, hopeless and sad. When a crew of volunteers rebuilt his kitchen, he said, "You gave me my life back." That's an expression of hope. He received more than a repaired kitchen. He received a renewed vision of his future because people cared enough to help him. He felt he was worth their effort, and he was no longer alone. Serving does that.

You have the ability to give hope to people in need. By doing what you can to serve them at their point of need, you help them see their future in a more positive, promising way. Your help does not have to be something overwhelming like providing employment to pull a woman out of poverty or rebuilding a home lost in a fire. Small acts of kindness do not require a major effort on your part—helping an elderly woman at the grocery story get groceries to her car, taking food to a neighbor who is recovering from surgery, spending time with a person who feels isolated—but they have the power to give hope and that makes all the difference.

A STORY OF SERVING

Mark was walking home from school one day when he noticed that a boy ahead of him had tripped and dropped all of the books he was carrying, along with two sweaters, a baseball bat, a glove, and a small tape recorder. Mark helped the boy pick up the scattered articles. Since they were going the same way, he helped the boy carry part of the burden. As they walked, he discovered the boy's name was Bill, that he loved video games, baseball, history, and that he was having lots of trouble with other subjects.

They arrived at Bill's home first and Mark was invited in for a Coke. The boys watched television and the afternoon passed pleasantly. After a few laughs and some small talk, Mark went home. Mark and Bill continued to see each other at school, had lunch together once in a while, and both graduated from junior high school. They ended up in the same high school where they had brief contacts over the years. Finally, the long-awaited senior year came, and three weeks before graduation, Bill asked Mark if they could talk.

He reminded Mark of the day years earlier when they had first met. "Did you ever wonder why I was carrying so many things home that day?" asked Bill. "You see, I cleaned out my locker because I didn't want to leave a mess for anyone else. I had stored away some of my mother's sleeping pills, and I was going home to commit suicide."

Bill told Mark that he realized he didn't want to die after spending time together talking and laughing. "I would have missed that time with you and many other good times in my life that followed. I am trying to say, Mark, that you did a lot more when you picked up those books that day. You saved my life."[29] Simple acts of service sometimes produce overwhelming results. Hope is among them.

---

29 Deana Landers Morningcoffeebeans.com/the-power-of-compassion, accessed May 27, 2021.

Chapter Six

SERVING BUILDS COMMUNITY

I am of the opinion that my life belongs to the whole community as long as I live. It is my privilege to do for it whatever I can. I want to be thoroughly used up when I die.
--GEORGE BERNARD SHAW

The life I touch for good or ill will touch another life, and in turn another, until who knows where the trembling stops or in what far place my touch will be felt.
--FREDERICK BUECHNER

Can you think of a time when the need for community was stronger than it is today? I have never seen a time when there was more divisiveness. I lived through the controversy and conflict surrounding the Vietnam War but even that, as bad as it was, does not compare to the divisiveness of the last few years. In his new book *Faithful Presence: The Promise and Peril of Faith* in the Public Square Former Tennessee Governor Bill Haslam says we are divided and angry.[30]

The great irony is that the one thing most people agree on is how divided we are! A recent survey found that eighty percent of Americans believe the country is "mainly" or "totally" divided.[31] That's eighty percent agreement on a single topic in a country that is split 50/50 on a wide range of issues. It's no longer just Republican vs. Democrat or liberal vs. conservative. It's the one percent vs. the ninety-nine percent, rural vs. urban, boomers vs. millennials. Climate doubters clash with believers. Bathrooms have become battlefields. Borders are battle lines. Sex and race, faith and ethnicity, on and on it goes.

BREAKDOWN OF COMMUNITY

Community in this context is the general sense of belonging and togetherness. Most of us have experienced this sense of community at one time or another in the past and perhaps we still do on occasion. *Community* means a sense of being accepted and supported by those who live in close proximity to us. It does not mean everyone agrees about everything but still manage to get along. Community is not utopia. It's a real place with real people who know each other and generally care for each other.

It seems this is what we have lost in recent years. That's not to say there are no places where genuine community still exists, but divisiveness has become pervasive and pernicious.

---

30 Bill Haslam, *Faithful Presence: The Promise and Peril of Faith in the Public Square.* Nashville: Nelson Books, 2021, p. 26.

31 https://www.nbcnews.com/politics/first-read/americans-are-divided-over-everything-except-division-n922511, accessed June 5, 2021.

There is hardly an aspect of life and relationships untouched by controversy and conflict. Consider how divided we have become:

Psychiatrist Richard Gillett includes this example in his book *It's a Freakin' Mess: How to Thrive in Divisive Times:*

> I have these neighbors, and I'd always had a nice cordial relationship with them. They were friendly and so was I. Then, a while ago, I saw the sign of the politician they were supporting on the edge of their lawn in good view of our road. I was shocked. My whole feeling toward them pretty well instantly changed. I found myself indignant and, I have to admit, angry. I told my wife about the sign.
>
> "How could they support that guy?" I said to her. "What's wrong with them?"
>
> Now, my wife and I were both upset.
>
> If I'm honest—and I'm not proud of this—I had contempt for these people. It was a horrible feeling to have. There was no pleasure in this feeling.
>
> And then, every time I saw their sign—which was every day—I felt bad. I even started to worry that drivers in the cars passing by might think that I shared the same political view as my neighbors.[32]

Political differences have divided neighborhoods. What was cordiality has become contempt. What was neighborliness has become self-imposed isolation for fear that disagreements will lead to a total breakdown of relationships.

---

32 Ricahard Gillett. *It's a Freakin' Mess: How to Thrive in Divisive Times.* Kingston Bridge Press', 2020, pp. 9-10.

Even church has become a place of division. The warmth of church fellowship has been a sanctuary from the hostilities reported every night on the evening news. Church was the one place we could go to get away from the divisiveness, not because everyone in church agrees about everything—far from it—but because relationships there have been valued above politics or cultural discord. Not necessarily. One church leader related that during the 2020 election another member asked who he supported for President. He declined to say because he felt his political persuasions are personal. The inquirer responded, "Well, if you don't support (naming one of the candidates), I don't think you are fit to hold the position you hold in the church."

Even close friends and families have felt the impact of political divisiveness. A 2017 Reuters/Ipsos poll revealed that one in six Americans had stopped talking to a family member or a close friend because of the 2016 election.[33] "I did straight up say, 'Dude, I'm done. Lose my number,'" said Sama Davis from Los Angeles, recalling when he "unfriended" a guy he'd been friends with since high school 25 years ago. Ricardo Deforest of Tampa conceded, "I hate to say it because family is everything," before somewhat angrily proclaiming, "I disowned them. In my mind they're

> "OTHERIZING IS THE DEVASTATING ABILITY WE HAVE TO VIEW DIFFERENT HUMAN BEINGS AS OTHER, OR AS NOTHINGS WHO ARE NOT WORTHY OF HUMAN COMPASSION OR CARE."

---

33 Haslam, p. 3.

not family anymore."[34] We are hardly surprised to hear such stories. If we have not personally experienced the same thing, we know someone who has. It's that bad, that widespread.

OTHERIZING

Like you, I shake my head and wonder how we got here; will we ever get back to civility and neighborliness? Richard Gillett uses the word *Otherizing* to describe what has happened: "*Otherizing* is the devastating ability we have to view different human beings as *other*, or as nothings who are not worthy of human compassion or care. The modern word otherize has not yet made the printed dictionaries, but it's already in all the online dictionaries."[35]

Politicians otherize their political rivals. We may disapprove or disagree with the level of hostility, but we are no longer surprised. Sadly, many everyday folks have adopted otherizing to promote their own viewpoints, dividing the political spectrum into *Us* and *Them*. Actually, it's more like *Us* Against *Them*. Unfortunately, media has joined the fray. I remember when the evening news was an unbiased source of information about national and international events. Few media outlets live up to that standard anymore. Add to this the incredible proliferation of social media with unchecked power to mold public opinion and we have a perfect storm for divisiveness.

It would appear that *otherizing* has reached epidemic levels. And the result has been a loss of community at every level.

---

34 https://www.nbcnews.com/politics/first-read/americans-are-divided-over-everything-except-division-n922511, accessed June 5, 2021.

35 Gillett, pp. 8-9.

How can we get it back? What can we do to turn this sad development around? Is there any hope for a better world?

SERVING IS THE TICKET

If, as I maintain, serving comes from humility, compassion, courage and a sense of responsibility, are not these the attributes that foster care for one another and build up community? Are they not on the opposite side of the relationship ledger from otherizing and criticism and alienation? Calls for civility and kindness are welcomed and encouraging but serving is kindness acted out. Serving comes from an attitude of kindness but takes kindness one step further by *doing* for others.

> " . . . SERVE ONE ANOTHER IN LOVE. THE ENTIRE LAW IS SUMMED UP IN A SINGLE COMMAND: 'LOVE YOUR NEIGHBOR AS YOURSELF.'

The biblical concept *one anothering* applies directly to the need for healthier relationships . It means to care for one another in any way and every way we can, to put others before self. The New Testament book of Galatians offers this advice: "serve one another in love. The entire law is summed up in a single command: 'Love your neighbor as yourself.' If you keep on biting and devouring each other, watch out or you will be destroyed by each other."[36] It would be hard to find another biblical passage so perfect for the conflict-riddled twenty-first century.

---

36 Galatians 5:13b-15, NIV.

One anothering is a good antidote for otherizing. When you see or hear otherizing, step in with one anothering and watch the temperature of the conflict go down. When you are on the receiving end of otherizing, look for ways to serve the source (the person or people) and watch the damaged relationship begin to heal.

Nowhere has the loss of community been so obvious than in race relations. The past year has seen the biggest surge in racial conflict in recent years sparking fresh outrage and adding fuel to the already raging fire of divisiveness in our nation. Each development—more deaths and more protests and stronger anger—widened the divide between blacks and whites, between political and cultural positions on both side of the debate. Because we've been here before and because divisiveness has become the order of the day, we can't help wondering if anything can bring races together in America.

Serving together has reunited the races in at least one small North Carolina community. A predominantly white congregation conducted a hugely successful Inasmuch event. Never had so many of their members served people in need in their community. Making plans for another serving event, they asked a black congregation to join them in serving the community. And that's what happened. Members of both congregations served happily together; afterwards, they celebrated their collaboration. In that celebration, one black woman said, "You white folks might not have noticed that my skin is lighter than that of my brothers and sisters, but they know it and they know why." She went on to tell that one of her ancestors was raped by a white man in the community. "It has taken putting on my work gloves and getting down on my hands and knees and working with some of your white folks to begin to let go of some of the bitterness I have felt for years."

Here's the rest of the story: a member of the white congregation died. His family knew he was a descendant of the man who had raped the black woman years earlier. When they planned his funeral, they invited the woman who spoke at the celebration, along with her family, to sit with the white family at the funeral! Serving together brought about reconciliation, not just for those families but for their entire community.

That's a unique situation, unlikely to be repeated, yet it shows the unifying power of serving. Serving others in need and serving alongside others to meet those needs promotes acceptance and mutual respect. We get to know each other more deeply when we are shoulder to shoulder working on a common task. What if our churches joined together--Black and White—to address the needs in their communities? I believe we would see the needle of racial conflict move in a positive direction and serving together would go a long way toward creating a healthier racial environment.

KEEP IT SIMPLE: STORIES OF BUILDING COMMUNITY

Popular TV host Fred Rogers of *Mr. Roger's Neighborhood,* known for his kindness, conflict avoidance, and community building, said, "The media shows the tiniest percentage of what people do. There are millions and millions of people doing wonderful things all over the world, and they're generally not the ones being touted in the news."[37]

---

37 https://www.inc.com/geoffrey-james/45-quotes-from-mr-rogers-that-we-all-need-today.html. Accessed June 1, 2021.

Perhaps we make the mistake of thinking divisiveness is so pervasive and the problems it creates are so overwhelming that only big solutions by powerful people will make a difference. I couldn't disagree more. In fact, I am convinced that ordinary people working alone or together will be to ones to bring back an authentic sense of community. It's people like Waffle House server, Evoni Williams, an eighteen-year-old in La Marque, Texas. In the din of a busy morning shift, one elderly customer—a man who eats at the Waffle House about once a week--waved down Evoni. She stopped what she was doing, went to him, and leaned over the counter to hear what he had to say. In a moment she straightened up, pulled the man's plate toward her, took his knife and fork and cut his food for him. He was not able to do that for himself as he was recovering from pneumonia and had a portable oxygen tank. Evoni Williams saw a need and met it. She thought nothing of it even though Evoni Williams is black and her customer is white. She never expected her simple act of kindness to go viral, but it did when another customer caught the whole thing on video and posted it on Facebook.[38]

It's people like the designers of the app *Nextdoor*, a twenty-first century substitute for back fence conversations between neighbors. It's an effective way to share information about recommended repair services, dog sitting, community news and needs, as well as a heads-up to suspicious behavior. The makers of Nextdoor have built into their site what they call a Kindness Reminder. If a member responds to a neigh-

---

38 https://www.usatoday.com/story/news/nation-now/2018/03/09/viral-photo-captures-heartwarming-moment-waffle-house-worker-helps-elderly-customer/409948002/ Accessed June 1, 2021.

bor's post with a potentially offensive or hurtful comment, Kindness Reminder will be prompted before the comment goes live. The member is given the chance to reference Nextdoor's Community Guidelines, reconsider or edit their reply, or ultimately refrain from posting it. Tests show that twenty percent of the people who saw the Kindness Reminder chose to edit their reply and negative comments were down overall.[39]

It's people like Jason Picanzo, a law enforcement officer with the Nashville Police Department. In 2018, the U.S. Justice Department asked the Nashville department to pilot a new style of community policing. This new approach sent officers to an over-policed community working to change the residents' perceptions of the police. Metro Nashville Police Department agreed to try this new approach and named Jason the leader of a team who would design ways to reach their objective. They identified a high crime area of Nashville known as "The Jungle" (named such by its residents). Shootings were commonplace along with drugs and other crimes. One resident said, "I went to the bathroom and all of a sudden I heard shots and got down on the floor and stayed there maybe forty-five minutes." Another said, "You can see where a shot came through my house right there. If I'd been standing there, I would have got shot in the head."

Jason's approach would be to serve the residents any way they could, earning their trust. "If we can serve these people, they will see who we really are, fellow citizens who just happen to wear a uniform," he said to his team. The team began walking through The Jungle looking for opportunities to en-

39 https://blog.nextdoor.com/2019/09/18/announcing-our-new-feature-to-promote-kindness-in-neighborhoods/ Accessed June 1, 2021.

gage residents who, naturally, were skeptical and stand-offish. Shortly, they encountered a seventy-year-old man who was sleeping on the floor of his apartment because he couldn't afford a bed. Jason and his team got him a bed. They found other residents who needed help with groceries so they provided food assistance and created a food pantry for the neighborhood stocked by a local church's monthly food drive. Jason and his team helped others with rent and even bought a used car for a resident who needed transportation to work.

One woman needed help with her utility bill and the Friends of Police organization paid her entire bill including late fees. They met a grandmother raising her twin five-year-old grandsons still sleeping in a crib because she couldn't afford beds for them. Jason's team got a set of bunk beds for the boys.

"We wanted to do something nice for the residents for helping us lower crime and being willing to work with us and we worked with a local church, our F.O.P., and a local business to pay for a cabana for the residents to sit in. The residents loved it and started hosting community cookouts under it and having birthday parties along with a number of other events," recalls Jason.

Results of the Nashville pilot program were amazing. Police calls declined by 17 percent. Violent crime declined by 40 percent. The biggest change was in the attitude of the residents toward the police:

"Everybody appreciates what y'all doing here.:

"Y'all took care of our neighborhood."

"I trust y'all highly."

"It's peaceful around here now. It's safe."

"We knew we had reached our objective of changing the residents' perceptions of us when there was a shooting and other cops went to investigate," Jason explained. They complained that no one in the neighborhood would talk to them. But when Jason's team came, the neighbors told them who did the shooting, why they did it, and where the drugs were. Furthermore, Jason has been to other police departments to share his experience and to encourage them to adopt serving people as the best way to build community.

What a powerful demonstration of serving people in need!

Chapter Seven

FIVE TRAITS OF A COMPASSIONARY

"Never underestimate the difference you can make in the lives of others. Step forward, reach out and help. This week reach out to someone that might need a lift."
--Pablo

Not everyone who serves is a servant. Not everyone who does something for someone else is serving.

Let me offer a personal example. If you were to Google "serving," you would see plenty of references to military service. I "served" for three years in the Army, but I do not think of that time as serving in the same sense as I've identified in previous chapters. If I had seen combat perhaps I would feel differently, but I had a desk job throughout my active duty. While I am proud to have served in the Army and reaped many benefits of that "service," I do not think of it as serving others. I worked at Fort Campbell, Kentucky processing soldiers who were absent without leave (AWOL) during the post-draft days of the all-volunteer Army. Many of those soldiers were unfit for the military and others simply did not want to be in the Army. When they were apprehended and brought to our facility, our officers made a judgment as to their fitness and/or likelihood to remain in the military and not leave unlawfully. My fellow legal clerks and I would process the necessary paperwork either to return them to duty or to discharge them. I did my job well, but I never once thought of what I was doing as serving.

Even now, when someone thanks me for my military service as often happens on Veterans Day or July 4th, I feel a little guilty because I didn't do anything special. My life was most certainly not on the line for my country. I had a job to do, and I did it. That's all.

We also refer to involvement in an organization as serving in that organization—the Book Club, the Historical Society, the Woodworkers Guild--but the nature of the organization may not involve doing for others. Joining an organization, paying dues, and participating in meetings is not serving. That's not to say these organizations have no value, just that involvement in a group does not amount to serving; it's giving your time and enjoying fellowship with like-minded folk, but it's not serving. Or course, some social clubs are involved in service projects. I joined a Rotary Club for a short time and was attracted to that particular group because one of their primary tenets is serving others. But, even then, I did not think of myself as serving. I enjoyed the camaraderie of the group and it was an opportunity to be with people outside my role as a minister.

So, let's clarify again what we mean by *serving*. First, it means reaching people at the point of their need—the hungry, the lonely, the imprisoned, the sick, the oppressed, the homeless, the mentally ill, the poor, and others.

Second, serving is an attitude that manifests itself in putting others before self, doing what you can to help with kindness and compassion whether or not they ask for help or even recognize their need of it. You might be serving fellow employees on the job by helping them resolve problems in their work or simply befriending them when they are dealing with personal issues. You might be serving neighbors in simple ways when they need help—putting out their trash when they are unable to do it themselves, taking care of their animals when they are away, or taking them a meal now and then. You may not necessarily see them as people in need, but these are ways to serve nonetheless.

I have already emphasized that anyone can serve. It does not require special skills or experiences, only a willingness to help others as you see the opportunity. I have helped mobilize thousands of volunteers in authentic service to their community and I have seen many people become servants in the best sense of the word. Out of this vast experience, I have identified five traits of a true servant or compassionary.

HUMILITY

Serving begins with humility. Some might argue that it begins with an opportunity—encountering a person in need—but without humility, you might not recognize the opportunity. At its base, serving is giving some of yourself to another--some of your time, some of your wisdom, some of your strength, some of your money. It is letting go of something in your possession for the benefit of others. To do that you have to see the other person as deserving or needing what you have to give. You have to believe that his needs take priority over your own, so you give your time. You have to believe that his needs are immediate and cannot be met financially or physically by the one in need, so you give your money. You have to believe that his needs cannot be met without additional resources, so you give your strength or offer your wise experience. Beneath every act of true service, regardless of the circumstances, is humility characterized by the willingness to put another's need above your own.

Humility is not an acquired skill. It is not something that can be *taught* as much as it can be *caught*. Humility is the willingness "to play second fiddle." The famous maestro Leonard Bernstein was once asked which instrument in an orchestra is the most difficult to play. "Second fiddle," he answered. "Yet, if we have no second fiddle, we have no harmony."

Humility is a virtue, not an achievement. Like a wet bar of soap, the more you squeeze it, the more likely it is to slip out of your hand. This slippery trait is hard to master—just when you think you've got it, your pride over such an achievement reminds you that humility is difficult to maintain. Consider the experience of Benjamin Franklin. He became concerned that he was not the best man he could be and he set out to remedy his situation. He was thoughtful and organized in his approach, identifying thirteen virtues he would attempt to master in his quest to be a better person: temperance, silence, order, resolution, frugality, industry, sincerity, justice, moderation, cleanliness, tranquility, chastity, and humility. Originally, Franklin had only twelve virtues on his list until a friend suggested he needed to work on humility! He would work on each virtue for one week, record his progress, move on to the next virtue. He made good progress and was quite pleased with himself until he came to humility. The more he worked on being humble, the farther it moved away from him. Finally, he had to admit that humility cannot be acquired; it's an inward, quiet way of seeing oneself in relation to others. He wrote in his autobiography, "Pride is so strong that you can probably spot it in these very autobiographical writings of mine, so look no further than this: For even if I could convince myself that I had overcome my pride, I should probably be proud of my humility."[40]

The problem with humility is not that we don't know what it is, but we live in a culture that devalues it, even ridicules it. Let a person exhibit humility on the job, especially if she is a leader, and you can be sure some will think less of her, criticize her, and treat her disrespectfully. In the business world, the way to impress others and gain their respect is to be bold and aggressive and confident. Humility doesn't stand a chance in that culture or among others with that mindset.

Humility is not . . . thinking less of yourself; it is thinking of yourself less.[41]

Humility is not . . . a sign of weakness.

Humility is not . . . sitting on the sideline.

Humility is . . . the courage to be honest with yourself and those around you.

---

40 Blaine McCormick, *Ben Franklin: America's Original Entrepreneur.* Entrepreneur Press, Canada, 2005, p. 128.

41 C.S. Lewis wrote: "Do not imagine that if you meet a really humble man he will be what most people think of 'humble' nowadays; he will not be a sort of greasy, smarmy person, who will always tell you, of course, he is nobody . . . . He will not be thinking about humility: he will not be thinking about himself at all." *Mere Christianity*

Humility is . . . being teachable.

Humility is . . . allowing yourself to be vulnerable.

SEEING NEEDS

A compassionary is one who truly sees the needs of others. Whether it's being observant or compassionate or simply open to being touched by another's need, I can't say. Frankly, it doesn't matter. Without sensing and seeing need, it is unlikely someone will serve. Before compassion leads to a helpful response, someone with vision has to see the need.

> "GREAT OPPORTUNITIES TO HELP OTHERS SELDOM COME, BUT SMALL ONES SURROUND US EVERY DAY."
>
> —SALLY KOCH

It's a common response from first-time volunteers—folks who have seldom if ever been involved in serving others in need: "I didn't realize how some people live" or "I didn't know how much some people struggle just to get along" or "I've lived here for years and never knew this was here." As they come face to face with people who are poor or homeless or hungry or neglected, something happens. Their spirit is stirred. Their heart is pricked. Their eyes are opened to the sad truth that some of their neighbors have real needs that they've never seen before.

A story from the life of Jesus illustrates the point. All four Gospels share the account of Jesus' dinner at a Jewish leader's home. During the evening, a woman "who had lived a sinful life"[42] came in and anointed his feet. As she cried, her tears wet Jesus' feet and she wiped them clean, anointing them with expensive perfume. The Jewish leaders present rebuked her and Jesus for allowing her intimate and costly act. In response to their criticism, Jesus told a parable that explained why the woman was so grateful and gracious to Jesus. Then he asked his critics a very important question: "Do you see this woman?" Jesus wasn't asking if they could see her as if their view was obstructed. He asked if they could see her for the needy person she was. Did they see her need?

The same question is appropriate for us; do we see the need? Unless we see, we will not serve. We encounter two problems with seeing needs. First, we don't see problems because we don't go to areas of need. Middle class Americans tend to travel in the same traffic patterns which rarely places them in the parts of the community where needs are more conspicuous. So, it's important to be intentional. These people are our neighbors but our paths seldom cross. We don't see them and we are not aware that they need what we can do for them.

I volunteer in the intake area of a local ministry that provides various services—assistance with rent or utilities, supplemental food, medical and dental referrals. I gather information about each client's circumstances including income and expenses. Both are meager and they seldom match. More than once I've recognized that more people need to sit where I sit when I am "on the job" because they have no idea how oth-

---

42 Luke's description of the woman. Don't be distracted by speculation as to what he means by 'sinful life' as some do. Simply know she was a woman who needed the acceptance and forgiveness Jesus could give her.

ers in our own community struggle to eke out a living. *More of my neighbors need to see the needs of our neighbors.*

If the first problem is lack of awareness, the second problem is lack of compassion. We don't want to see. We turn away. How many times have you grimaced and looked away from television commercials which feature pictures of emaciated children? How much worse when we turn away from poverty-stricken families or under-nourished children we see in person! Do you look away from the ragged, dirty person on the street corner holding a sign that says, "Anything will help."? Do you try to avoid eye contact so you will not feel guilty?

A compassionary has vision; her eyes are wide open to needs around her. Even if seeing needs is often painful, a compassionary does not look away but allows herself to be moved toward serving.

COMPASSION

Did you expect that compassion would be first on a list of traits of compassionaries? That's understandable, but I listed humility first because I am convinced that it is impossible to find a person who serves in an authentic way who does not have humility. An attitude of intentionally and naturally putting others before self is the basis of serving. The ability to see others'

SYMPATHY IS PITY, FEELING REGRET BUT WITHOUT THE DESIRE TO ALLEVIATE THE OTHER PERSON'S PAIN. EMPATHY IS WHEN YOU FOREGO JUDGMENT FOR UNDERSTANDING, WHEN YOU MOVE OUT TO HELP INSTEAD OF BLAMING.

needs is a close second to humility, so that moves compassion down the list.

Compassion is being moved by another's pain or need. The role model for compassion is the biblical story of the Good Samaritan. In telling the story, Jesus noted that when the Samaritan saw the robbery victim on the side of the road, "he had compassion on him." His heart went out to the wounded man. As Martin Luther King, Jr. said, "The Samaritan asked not what would happen to him if he stopped to help, but what would happen to the man if he did not stop."

Compassion is what leads us to respond to another's need. Often, that response is so quick it's hard to know which comes first: seeing the need or feeling compassion. This trait is grounded in empathy or the ability to put oneself into another's situation as if it were his own. Empathy is when you put yourself in the lives of others. It's when you truly understand their pain, joy, fears and actions. By the way, empathy is not the same as sympathy, nor is compassion. Sympathy is pity, feeling regret but without the need or desire to do anything to alleviate the other person's pain. Empathy is when you forego judgment for understanding, when you move out to help instead of blaming. Henry Ford said, "Never look down on anybody unless you're helping him up."[43]

Stories of compassion abound. Here's another personal one. I lost my wife of forty years suddenly and tragically ten years ago. I was devasted, depressed and perpetually sad. I knew I needed to do something to get out of that dark place. Before my wife died, we had promised her sister we would

43 www.motivationalwellbeing.com/55-meaningful-quotes-about-helping-others , accessed June 7, 2021.

visit her in Glacier National Park over the summer. She had applied to work in one of the park's mountaintop camps and we were planning to make the trip if she got the job. My wife's death put our promise in question. Finally, I decided I wanted to go; I was convinced it would do me good to get away and enjoy the incredible scenery. I asked my friend Wayne Byrd if he would consider going with me. At first, he declined thinking he couldn't afford the trip, but a few days later, he called to say he wanted to join me. I was elated. The trip gave me something to look forward to. A good friend made the trip even better.

Wayne and I flew to Montana and proceeded to haul ourselves and our gear about twelve miles up the mountain. I was in pretty good shape from a cycling routine so the hike up the mountain wasn't too bad for me, but it was a real challenge for Wayne who had not been exercising. Through grit and determination, he made it to the top. We enjoyed three incredible days going all the way to the very top of one mountain. I will never forget the incredible views and the moments that my spirit began to heal. More importantly, I will never forget what Wayne did for me. When I needed a friend, when I needed company the most, he was there for me. His compassion toward me will always be the reason I love Wayne Byrd like a brother.

COURAGE

Inevitably, accepting an opportunity to serve will move you out of your comfort zone. Uncomfortable requests, dangerous communities, unstable relationships—these and more unexpected situations require the courage of your convictions to bolster your resolve to serve. Of course, there are times and circumstances which require professional intervention and your commitment to serve others has to take a backseat to personal or situational safety. But a compassionary may often be called on to face her fears and step out courageously. A homeless person in a shelter where you volunteer needs transportation to a pharmacy to get a prescription filled--is it safe to give this stranger a ride? A teenager at the school where you volunteer shares that she doesn't feel safe at home. Her father has never been around; her mother has multiple men into the home and some of the men look menacingly at the teenager. She asks for help to find a safe place to stay, at least temporarily. Your compassion kicks into high gear and your heart goes out to her—is this girl's problem beyond your ability and responsibility? You can't fix this situation. You can sympathize and if you allow yourself to be vulnerable, you may be able to empathize, but there are limits to what you can do as a school volunteer. There are rules and your continued service will be jeopardized if you violate them.

Serving others sometimes requires courage coupled with discernment. If a situation is too risky, it may be time to step back. If you're simply out of your comfort zone and there's no real danger, then you may need to summon the courage to serve. The fact is when you give yourself in response to another's need, you become vulnerable to their pain and you may feel inadequate or out of control.

A compassionary is one who pushes past fear to serve whether that fear is real or perceived danger or merely discomfort from unfamiliar circumstances. Fear can paralyze us. It can trump feelings of compassion and cause us to ignore needs we can plainly see out of a sense of self-protection.

Self-protection is natural and works to our benefit, but there are times when we can set it aside for something we believe is more important. A compassionary is able to do that.

The example of Mother Teresa and her Sisters of Charity serving lepers in India comes to mind. But that example is too heroic, too off-the-charts for most of us, so I prefer to offer a more "common" example. Under the cruel oppression of the Taliban, women in Afghanistan were forced to wear a *burqa*, a cloak that covers everything but the woman's eyes. Women were considered property, young girls were sold into slavery to pay family debts, girls were forbidden to go to school or attend college. In recent years, as the Taliban's influence has reduced, stories of courageous defiance are being shared.

One hero of these stories is Mrs. Zubeida, the wife of a doctor. Mrs. Zubeida taught in a flourishing network of illegal, underground schools. She set up her school above her husband's office, secretly teaching hundreds of girls to read and write. When the Taliban would come to investigate, she blamed the noise on her husband's patients. When the Taliban got too close, she would change the time and place of the lessons. Had they been caught, Mrs. Zubeida and her band of outlaw teachers would have been severely beaten. If her students had been found with books in their possession, they would have been punished as well. But she never thought of quitting. "I had to help my country," Mrs. Zubeida says. "The girls love to study. They want to be educated. They have lots of wishes and lots of hope."[44] Mrs. Zubeida acted with courage

---

44 *Connections: The newsletter of ideas, resources and information for homilists and preachers.* Londonderry NH: Media Works, December 2002, p. 2.

in the face of many dangers to serve the Afghani women and girls.

SENSE OF RESPONSIBILITY

A popular pastor of a large Chicago church challenged his congregation to get involved in serving others. He used the metaphor of a game--players on the field and spectators filling the stands watching the game. He encouraged his parishioners to get out of the stands and onto the field. Stop merely watching others who serve, he suggested, and "get in the game."

> "STEP-UP, GET-UP,
> SHOW-UP, LISTEN-UP
> AND GROW-UP."
> —LOUISE JACKSON

This is a good segue into the final characteristic of a true servant--a sense of responsibility. I have observed that people who "get in the game", who respond to the opportunity to serve others in need, feel responsible—not responsible for the pain or suffering of others, but responsible to do something to meet their need or alleviate their suffering.

A sense of responsibility can come from two primary sources: a strong sense of community and obedience to God. Responsibility comes when you recognize that you are part of a larger community and you want to make it a better place to live. So, you pay your taxes, obey the laws, participate in community events, and do what you can to serve the less fortunate. Serving is one more way you try to be a good citizen.

For people of faith, being responsible in ways that serves others is a matter of obedience to God. Even a cursory reading of the Bible, shows that God has a special place in his heart for the poor, the oppressed, those on the margins of society, and victims of injustice. Micah 6:8 succinctly outlines God's expectation that his people will serve others: "What does the Lord require of you? To act justly and to love mercy and to walk humbly with your God." Serving is a matter of faithfulness to God's expectations.

A sense of responsibility can help overcome feeling overwhelmed by so many needs that you don't know where to start. If all you see is the big picture--millions of hungry people or hundreds of homeless people in your community or countless children living in unsafe conditions--it's easy to be overwhelmed and paralyzed into inaction. However, a sense of responsibility can help you see that you can make a difference for some. You may not be able to end world hunger, but you can get food to one hungry family. You cannot save the thousands of victims of sex trafficking, but you can work with a local agency to get a few young women off the streets and into a safer life. Each and every person can do *something*.

Marketing guru Seth Godin puts it this way: "You can't change the world, but you can change five people. Why don't you just change five people today? Because if you change five people today, you will be able to change six people tomorrow, and then you're on your way—because most people change *nobody.* . . . You don't need a permit to change someone. You just need to care."[45]

These five traits of a true servant—humility, seeing needs, compassion, courage, and a sense of responsibility--are not

---

45 Hanbury, Aaron Cline. "Want to Change the World: Seth Godin Knows How." Relevant. Issue 81: May/June 2016 as cited by Mark Maxwell, *Networking Kills: Success Through Serving.* Desolation Row Press, Nashville, 2018, p. 73.

meant to be a test of fitness for serving. Rather, these traits will enhance your understanding of what moves people to serve and to overcome obstacles to serving. Furthermore, I do not offer this list as though each characteristic stands alone. At their best these traits work together. Humility puts others before self and vision enables one to see others' needs. Compassion moves you to act, courage helps you to set aside fears. And a sense of responsibility provides additional motivation to get involved. Working together in community with others also provides opportunities to lead in the areas where you are strongest and to follow and learn from those who exhibit the characteristics you most need to develop. Author Maya Angelou was noted for saying, "It takes a village to raise a child." It takes a community of servers to meet the needs of others.

In the midst of street fighting as part of a larger war, a news reporter covering the battle, saw a child wander into the line of fire and get shot. Forgetting his job, he risked his own life to run to the injured child, scoop him up, and dash to safety. He saw that the child's wound was serious and required immediate attention, so he carried the child around the corner, flagged down a cab driver, jumped into the back seat, and said, "Hospital, please hurry!!" As the cab sped toward the closest hospital, the reporter kept saying to the driver, "Faster! My child is dying! My child is dying!" At the hospital's Emergency Room entrance the reporter jumped out of the cab and passed off the child to the waiting arms of a nurse. The cab driver got out of his cab, too, wanting to be sure he had gotten the child to emergency care in time.

After he composed himself, the reporter asked the cabbie to take him back to the neighborhood where the fighting took place. He said, "I have to go tell his parents what has happened." Perplexed the cabbie responded, "But you said, 'my child is dying.'" The reporter replied, "They're all our children."

Serving Model #2

SEDUCED BY THE POOR

How do you know when God tells you to do something? Does it come in an audible voice? Some say so. Does it come in a twist of events that have no other logical explanation? Some say so. Does it come through a classified ad as was the case for Tom Steele? Possibly. If you were Sarah and Bill, you could say divine instruction comes when two people are told to do the same thing completely independent of each other.

Sarah was volunteering with Bridge Refugee Services—an organization that assists refugees to resettle in the United States—when God told her to move to a part of her community where she could serve refugees more effectively. Bridge helps with temporary housing, food, clothing and other necessities as well as jobs, school enrollment, and completion of government documents with the goal of finding permanent housing for refugees. Sarah was happily engaged in this program when she and a friend attended a conference on working with refugees.

As they drove home, Sarah and her friend discussed the conference. Her friend asked Sarah for her takeaway from the conference. "God told me to move my family to a community where there are a number of refugees so I can serve them better," Sarah responded. One of the conference speakers had deeply touched Sarah with this statement, "You can't minister to people unless you can get to them in your bare feet."

Almost immediately Sarah was anxious about telling her husband Bill about this revelation. He supported Sarah's work with refugees but she was about to take it to a whole new level. That night she gently broached the subject. When she said, "God told me to do something this week," Bill responded, "I know. We need to move to a community where there is a large number of refugees." Before Sarah could describe her experience at the conference, Bill told her about his visit with a patient in the hospital where he serves as chaplain. He described how God spoke to him, telling him that he and his family should take up residence in a particular low-income community in their town. Sarah's anxiety was replaced by shock and joy that both she and Bill had received the same message totally independently of each other.

Sarah and Bill's inspiring experience is not unique; many of their life experiences prepared them to respond quickly and favorably to this special call to deepen their service to refugee families. As newlywed seminarians, they were introduced to Tony Campolo, a popular prophet of the latter twentieth century, through tapes of his sermons. Sarah says one phrase that stuck with them from Campolo's messages was being "seduced by the poor." Campolo was referring to an addictive attraction that sometimes happens when people build relationships with people in need. Sarah explains that their value system has been shaped by the idea of always living within their means; they seldom purchase anything new—cars, clothing or other necessities. Relocating to a low-income community was not as much of a stretch as it might be for other middle-class families. Sarah and Bill would say their life journey and values set them up to be seduced by the poor.

In 2005, they moved with their middle-school aged daughter into a diverse community that is one-third African American, one-third Hispanic, and one-third "other" (a blend of white, Asian, Indian and other nationalities). One hundred percent of the school children in this community qualify for free lunches. Sarah and Bill bought a dilapidated home and set about making it livable for their family. They have faced challenges along the way but in every case God has provided.

One of the most difficult aspects of their decision was the push back from church friends. Some were openly critical. One close friend accused Sarah of being a bad mother to move her daughter into the "unsafe and undesirable part of town." However, as Sarah has shared her experiences, some of those same friends have become supportive. Several now volunteer at the school where Sarah serves. Her commitment has been contagious and together they are making a difference in the school and community.

Another surprise has been the push back Sarah and Bill have received from residents in the community. Some resent their involvement and misinterpret their serving as an attempt to control the community. Sarah and Bill are frustrated by this response but believe perseverance and faithfulness will win out. Interestingly, she says they feel like missionaries in no-man's land, with opposition from all sides, but Sarah is resolute in her belief that serving the people of her community will prove her sincerity and love. Sarah continues to affirm her response to a critical friend, "God told me to do this and I'm going to do it no matter what you say." When a person is seduced by the poor, it lasts a long time. Such is the experience of compassionaries.

PART THREE

Chapter 8

MERCY IS MESSY

We need to redefine ministry. Ministry is simply
"meeting another's need with the resources
God has given to you." That's enough of a definition
to get us started exploring the possibilities.
--RICK RUSAW

It's a good story…without a happy ending. Joe was homeless having battled alcoholism and the consequences of his disease for years. Whenever Joe got to the point that he needed help to survive, he would go to a church or another helping agency hoping they would have mercy on him. Once when he went to a church for help, his visit took an unexpected turn. He asked for a few dollars for a meal. The man at church (I'll call him Sam) gave Joe a few bucks and then he did something no one else had ever done when Joe asked for help: Sam invited Joe to church. "You know," Sam said, "there are a lot of caring people in this church who would welcome you if you came. I'll pick you up next Sunday if you'll come." Joe was so surprised that he agreed to go to Sam's church.

On Sunday, Sam showed up to get Joe and they went to Sam's church where he introduced Joe to his friends. Surprised again, Joe found them genuinely warm and friendly even though he felt out of place in his grungy street clothes while they were in their Sunday best. Joe came back the next Sunday and the next and the next. Slowly, he formed relationships with Sam's Sunday school class. Eventually, he was given the job of making coffee for the class, a job he took seriously. It made him feel more included since he had some responsibility.

The entire class took Joe under their wings. They took him to lunch after church most Sundays. They helped him get an apartment in government-subsidized housing and got him a cell phone so they could stay in touch. Occasionally, Joe lapsed back into his self-destructive dependence on alcohol. Sam took the lead in helping Joe, arranged counseling and rehab, hoping that with the support of the class it would be enough to get Joe onto a positive path. When Joe "fell off the wagon" a few times, some class members went to their pastor to express frustration about Joe. "I care about Joe. I genuinely hope he gets his life together and I am proud of what you've done for him," said their pastor, "but, frankly, I'm more concerned about what Joe can teach us about serving others than I am about whether he turns his life around."

With that prophetic statement, the class redoubled their efforts to help Joe make better decisions and do more to help himself. Sadly, Joe was unable to keep his small apartment; he was given several warnings and improved for a while but would fail to meet even the minimum standards of cleanliness. Finally, he was told he had to leave so he went back to the streets. He stopped attending church, and he lost his cell phone and the connections it provided. Joe was right back where he was when he first met Sam.

This example illustrates one of the great frustrations of serving those in need—mercy is messy. The fact is when you serve people in need, you do not always get your preferred outcome. It's naïve to think everyone will respond as we expect or prefer; not everyone will use our help as momentum to move in a more positive direction. Serving people at their point of need offers hope, but not everyone we serve recognizes that hope or acts on it in healthy ways.

What are we to do with the messiness of mercy? How can we cope with the frustrations that are bound to surface when our best intentions turn out badly? How can we keep those frustrations from hindering our serving? Any book on serving that does not deal with the frustrations that are common with helping others is not complete. So, I want to take a shot at what you can do to manage at least these aspects of the messiness of mercy: ingratitude, being taken advantage of, and enabling.

INGRATITUDE

One of the "payoffs" of helping others is the "thank you" we get. Depending on the circumstances, it may be a tearful expression of gratitude, accompanied by a heartfelt handshake or hug. It may be a meek but sincere verbal expression delivered quietly and without a physical touch, not even eye contact sometimes. Whether or not we expect it, any expression of gratitude makes us feel good, but there are times when there is no expression of thanks. This is the exception, not the rule, but we usually notice when someone we've helped fails to say thanks. Most people do not help others expecting thanks in return, but the fact is thanking others for even the smallest gesture of kindness or politeness (holding the door for someone as they enter/exit a building, allowing them to get in a queue before you, etc.) is so common that we do expect it. When it isn't offered, we notice whether or not we think about it beyond the moment.

Jesus noticed. On one occasion Jesus healed ten lepers.[46] Only one came back to thank him. Jesus asked where the other nine were, not because he expected to be thanked but because gratitude was an indication of a humble spirit in those who were healed. I don't believe Jesus was offended that only one person came back to express his gratitude. However, he noted that the one who did was a Samaritan (or half-Jew). By the culture of the time, Jesus' followers would have excluded Samaritans and would have had little expectation that a Samaritan would behave "appropriately." This is just one of several times when Jesus' actions or his parables included those who showed more faith than those who might have been expected to act faithfully (as a proper Jewish citizen).

At the worst, ingratitude can sour a person's willingness to serve. A quick internet search of how to handle ingratitude when helping others contained a surprising number of comments suggesting "ingrates" should be stricken from the list of people to be helped. Perhaps there could come a time when repeated experiences of ingratitude might lead to discontinuing assistance, but there would be fewer home-

---

46 Luke 17:11-19.

less shelters and food pantries if that became a widespread practice.

I offer this help in dealing with ingratitude while serving others. First, check your intent. Are you serving to make yourself feel good by hearing a thank you or are you serving because of a need you can meet? Are you serving because you believe you have a responsibility to share with others, or are you helping because you enjoy the "helper's high"?

Second, have compassion for the situation of the person you are serving. Often, people who need help find themselves in circumstances that are embarrassing. For example, many who lost jobs during the pandemic may have visited a food pantry for the first time, swallowing their pride to do so. And it may very well be that their pride was still stuck in their throat when they received free food and were unable to say thank you.

> HAVE COMPASSION FOR THE SITUATION OF THE PERSON YOU ARE SERVING. OFTEN, PEOPLE WHO NEED HELP FIND THEMSELVES IN CIRCUMSTANCES THAT ARE EMBARRASSING.

We may not be aware of it, but many people in need feel shame when they have to ask for help. (Fortunately, many of us who volunteer to serve others have never been in a situation where we have to ask for help.) A recent study in Australia, based on in-depth interviews with twenty-four volunteers providing charity and fifty-seven people receiving charity, found that people receiving charity felt shame from the judgments of volunteers and from the position of passively receiving what is given.[47] A person feeling shame may not be inclined to express his thanks or may not remember this common courtesy.

Resentment may also be wrapped up in the feelings of people in need—resentment because they do not have as much as others, because life is not fair, because forces beyond their control have forced them into a position of need. Resentment is a form of anger and anger is not on our list of expectations when we serve others. Nevertheless, anger and resentment may come. When you sense the people you are serving are feeling resentful, the most helpful thing you can do is listen. Shut up and listen! No commentary needed. Chances are they do not resent you for helping them and listening will make that clear. They may be justified in their resentment; they may be victims of injustice or unfairness, so anger in the form of resentment is normal. If some resentment stems from their perception that you have more than they have, the best thing you can do is agree. Say something like, "You know what, I think I would feel the same way if our places were swapped." You may be surprised at their response.

Listening is a necessary skill for anyone who serves people in need. Nothing conveys caring as well as listening, regardless of the circumstances. Truly listening to another person not only helps you understand that person's life situation, but also helps the person unburden himself about his pain. Listening is the one thing any person can do to help another anywhere any time.

---

47 Cameron Parsell, "Charity and Shame: Toward Reciprocity." Social Problems, spaa057 https://doi.org/10.1093/socpro/spaa057, published 21 October, 2020, accessed June 10, 2021.

A friend told me of a time when he worked with a company to assess damages to personal property after a disaster. He remembers standing with a family whose home was totally destroyed by a tornado. Everything they owned was gone. They were crying and wondering out loud how they were going to put their life back together. My friend listened to them. He was there to do a job for his employer and ultimately the family in the process of filing and awarding insurance claims, but he took the time to listen to the people pour our their hearts in fear and grief from their incredible losses. Listening is an indispensable part of serving.

BEING TAKEN ADVANTAGE OF

If you serve people in need long enough, you will eventually encounter a situation in which you are taken advantage of. The person asking for help misrepresents himself and his need in order to get what he wants. More often than not, what he wants is money. If he gets what he wants, he looks for ways to get more. If the person asking for help is inclined to maximize what he can get, asking and giving can go on for a while until the well runs dry. Then he moves on to another well.

How do you deal with situations where you are taken advantage of? If it happens often enough, it is easy to become jaded about serving at all. I offer these suggestions for ways to deal with times when your good will has been abused. First, go easy on yourself. No one gets it right all the time. Being taken advantage of does not mean you are gullible or an easy mark. It may mean your compassion supersedes your need to be right. The help you gave was not wasted. God looks at the heart of the servant not the outcome of his serving. Look for better ways to verify needs. Don't hesitate to take some time to respond to repeated requests for assistance and look for alternative answers rather than responding with the same answer even if the request is the same. Other avenues of help may be an alternative route and you may need to direct the person to another resource.

A friend in the serving "business" has had to learn how to cope with the frustrations of helping people who don't always want to be helped, or at least in the ways that are most helpful for them. On the issue of being taken advantage of, she says, "You don't have to know the end of the story; just that you are part of their journey to hope."[48] Remember, you probably don't know all of the information about the person or his situation and what you think is most helpful may not be the only positive option. Roger Von Ech in his book, *A Whack on the Side of the Head,* suggests that when one answer isn't well received we look for "the second right answer."

ENABLING

Enabling is making it possible for a person to continue in a self-destructive lifestyle. Giving money to a person with an addiction makes it possible for her to continue her addiction, removing consequences of bad decisions in the name of helping, but in fact prolonging a person's dependence on others for survival. One friend who has served the homeless in her community effectively for several years encourages those who serve to refrain from giving money to homeless persons because she has seen them spend it on drugs and alcohol and

---

48 Sue Byrd, Director Emeritus, Fayetteville Area Operation Inasmuch, Fayetteville, North Carolina in a personal conversation with the author.

other unhealthy habits. "I used to give money with the best of intentions until I became convinced I was enabling my friends to keep up their self-destructive ways," she confesses.

Serving becomes enabling when we do not include the people we are helping in their own solutions to their problems. Enabling promotes entitlement. Entitlement is the belief that I am supposed to be served or taken care of, the more the better. I deserve whatever I can get. Entitled people take little or no responsibility for themselves. Entitlement is the enemy of self-improvement.

> ENABLING IS OFTEN DISGUISED AS HELPING, BUT IT'S QUITE THE OPPOSITE. ENABLING CREATES A SENSE OF POWERLESSNESS, OFTEN DISCOURAGING AND DEMOTIVATING THE PERSON WHO NEEDS HELP.

Enabling more often occurs in long-term situations of serving— within families, in work relationships, or in on-going assistance. "Enabling is often disguised as helping, but it's quite the opposite. Enabling creates a sense of powerlessness, often discouraging and demotivating the person who needs help."[49] If you wonder if your attempts to help have crossed over into the territory of enabling, here are some questions to consider:

- Are my actions helping this person to feel more self-empowered?

---

49 Nea Joy, "When Helping Hurts: A Lesson on Enabling," https://possibilitychange.com/when-helping-hurts-a-lesson-on-enabling/ accessed June 10, 2021.

- Are his circumstances staying the same, worsening or improving?
- Is this person doing his absolute best to help himself?
- Are my actions motivated by fear? Pity? Guilt?
- Am I helping this person to take advantage of her full potential?
- What good has come from my help?
- What harm has come from my help?[50]

What happened to Joe whose story was told at the beginning of this chapter? I don't know because I've lost contact with him. I was among those who helped him from time to time, taking him to doctor's appointments or to lunch. I was as disappointed as anyone when I learned he'd lost his apartment and gone back to the streets.

Remember the pastor's response to the frustration about Joe's inability to get his life going in the right direction? What did the church learn about serving from their experiences with Joe? They learned that mercy is messy. Not every case of serving is a success story, at least not in the ways we usually think of success. Maybe success means something different when it comes to serving. Maybe it doesn't have to mean the person is "healed" of all his pain or rehabilitated from his poor life choices. Maybe it means the one serving has given of himself generously with the sincere hope and prayer that people like Joe will come around to the truth that he has to help himself in order to have a better life. Maybe it means that service rendered is authentic, that it comes from humility and

---

50 Joy, accessed June 10, 2021.

compassion regardless of the outcome. We will never stop wanting our serving to help make people's lives better, and we shouldn't, but we *always* serve without control over the circumstances that put people in need. Remember what my friend said, "You don't have to know the end of the story; just that you have been part of their journey to hope." And consider this quote from Mother Teresa, "Do things for people not because of who they are or what they do in return, but because of who you are."[51]

---

51 parade.com/1246359/marynliles/mother-teresa-quotes/ accessed May, 2021.

Chapter Nine

TO BE OR NOT TO BE A GOOD SAMARITAN

*Like the Good Samaritan, may we not be ashamed
of touching the wounds of those who suffer,
but try to heal them with concrete acts of love.*
—POPE FRANCIS

See if this sounds familiar. I was driving down the highway when I saw someone very slowly driving on the shoulder of the road. As I got closer, I saw their left rear tire was flat. They were cautiously trying to make it to an upcoming exit to stop and maybe get help in changing the tire. When I passed them, I thought to myself, *"Why didn't I stop to help? That driver may not have known how to change a tire and I could have done that."*

Feelings of guilt washed over me as I continued on my way. In fact, my guilt may have been stronger than most. After all, I work with a ministry that equips churches to mobilize their members to serve people in need. I preach about it, write about it (this book and a bi-weekly blog), dream about it:

serving people in need has become the focus of my life. *What a louse I am*, I thought. *What a hypocrite!*

In Chapter 10 I will address common reasons people say they are reluctant to serve people in need. For now, let me just say fear plays a big role in that reluctance—fear of getting in over one's head, fear of the unknown element in serving strangers, fear of an uncomfortable or potentially risky situation. Stopping to assist someone who appears to need help is a common occurrence and concern about doing so is widespread. Given that continuing discussion and the debate about the wisdom of intervention in potentially dangerous situations, I want to treat this concern about serving with special care.

It's not hard to find people who argue that it is unwise to stop on the road to help someone who appears to be stranded or in difficulty. Likewise, it's not hard to find others who argue just as vigorously that we should not refuse to help just because we don't know what might happen. When stories of "Good Samaritans" include harm coming to the helper—being injured or robbed or otherwise mistreated--the debate rages anew about whether to risk harm to help strangers along our way. I have no illusions about resolving this debate, but I do want to weigh in on it and leave you to make your own decision.

First, let's review the term "Good Samaritan". Jesus told the parable of the Good Samaritan when a scholar in Jewish law approached him asking what he had to do to have eternal life. Jesus asked the scholar to identify the core of the Jewish law: "Love the Lord your God with all your heart and with all your soul and with all your strength and with all your mind" and "Love your neighbor as yourself," he responded. Jesus agreed and the man asked, "Who is my neighbor?" Jesus's answer has become one of the best-known stories ever told—the parable of the Good Samaritan.

Here's the story, updated for today:

A man was traveling from Jerusalem to Jericho when he was attacked by robbers. They beat him, robbed him, and left him to die. Soon, a priest came by and even though he saw the man, he hurried on without stopping to help. Later a preacher happened by. He saw the victim, and he, too, went on his way without stopping. Even later, a black man came that way. (For Jesus's audience, a Samaritan was a cultural outsider for whom they had little or no regard: depending on who's hearing this parable today, the "Samaritan" could be black or an Islamic jihadist or an BLM activist or anyone else who's help would be unexpected or even unwanted.) When he saw the man lying beside the road, bloody, beaten, almost naked and near death, he had compassion on the man, and he stopped. He did what he could to bind up the man's wounds, put him on his own donkey, and took him to a hotel. He paid for several day's lodging and told the clerk he would be back in a week; if he owed any more, he would pay it.

When Jesus finished the parable, he asked his inquiring Jewish scholar which of the three men was a neighbor to the victim by the road and the scholar answered, "The one who had mercy on him." Jesus's response? "Go and do likewise." Our common cultural reference to the "good Samaritan" comes directly from this parable and the scholar's answer is precisely what the term means today—someone who stops to help a person in need, who shows mercy to a stranger. Now you know.

ASKING THE RIGHT QUESTION

When deciding whether to stop to help someone in need, it matters what questions we ask. What will happen to me if I stop? Is there danger here I cannot see? Will the help I give be misused?

Why didn't the priest or preacher (Levite) in Jesus' parable not stop to help? Jesus doesn't tell us but from what we know of Jewish culture in the first century, they may have been concerned about being defiled by the wounded man. Touching this wounded man would have rendered them ceremonially unclean and therefore unable to carry out their religious responsibilities. Perhaps they were in a hurry and would be late for an important appointment if they stopped. Perhaps they were afraid or repulsed by the sight of the man's injuries.

> THE QUESTION THE PRIEST AND LEVITE ASKED WAS *"IF I STOP TO HELP THIS MAN, WHAT WILL HAPPEN TO ME?"* THE SAMARITAN REVERSED THE QUESTION: *"IF I DO NOT STOP TO HELP THIS MAN, WHAT WILL HAPPEN TO HIM?"*
>
> —MARTIN LUTHER KING, JR.

The best insight into this parable comes from Martin Luther King, Jr. He said the first question the priest and Levite asked was, "If I stop to help this man, what will happen to me?" The Samaritan reversed the question: "If I do not stop to help this man, what will happen to him?" Asking the right question made all the difference.

TO SERVE IS TO BE VULNERABLE

We are averse to risk. We live in a culture that promotes self-protection--lock your car, avoid interaction with strangers, carry your keys in your hand in case you need quick entry into your car or a quick weapon, be aware of your surroundings at all times. We don't just lock our doors, we install a video security system. When we're home, we're safe but when we're away, our stuff is safe.

Without a doubt, we live in a more dangerous world than it was a few decades ago. Security has become a higher priority than it was for my parents or grandparents. Our fear of risk is a boon to the billion-dollar security business. But risk aversion is a barrier to serving.

THE BIBLICAL VIEW OF SERVING IS TO GIVE OF YOURSELF TO ANOTHER WITHOUT REGARD TO SAFETY. AUTHENTIC SERVING INCLUDES SOME LEVEL OF VULNERABILITY.

Another way to talk about risk is in terms of vulnerability. If serving leads to risk and if serving requires us to push past the risk, then serving is a matter of allowing ourselves to be vulnerable. In her popular TED talk, "The Power of Vulnerability," Brene' Brown shares her discovery that vulnerability actually gives people a stronger sense of purpose and enhances their relationships. Years of research has confirmed that vulnerability is the key to authenticity. Brown found that people who allow themselves to be vulnerable "believe what makes them vulnerable also makes them beautiful."[52] Authen-

---

52 Brene' Brown, TED Talk, accessed June 5, 2021.

ticity enables us to make meaningful connections with people and produces deep feelings of joy.

Can you see how being vulnerable can contribute to an attitude of serving? Allowing ourselves to be exposed to risk lends credibility to serving. Most serving does not require much vulnerability, but sooner or later we may encounter a need that requires more than we anticipated. That's when compassion must be stronger than vulnerability. It was true for the Samaritan in Luke 10, and it's true for us today. The biblical view of serving is to give of yourself to another without regard to safety. Serving is not a matter of convenience nor of being blessed by our service. Authentic serving includes some level of vulnerability.

THE REST OF THE STORY

This chapter began with a personal story of failure to serve when I chose not to stop to help a motorist with a flat tire. I felt guilty about not stopping, sufficiently guilty to say a short prayer asking God to forgive me and promising that if he would give me another opportunity, I would not pass by again. Less than thirty minutes down the road, I saw another stopped motorist. I exited at my first opportunity, turned around, went back and asked if I could help. He was pouring gas into his vehicle and said he was okay, but he thanked me for stopping. We talked a few minutes and eventually, I went on my way without doing anything to help him. Nevertheless, he was grateful I stopped, and I was, too. When he thanked me for stopping, he noted that people don't do that anymore. As a former truck driver, he had seen plenty of instances in which people refused to stop.

So, I didn't help him. Or did I? If you think only of the material help the man needed—gas for his car—maybe not. But if you think of the encouragement my presence gave him, maybe so. He was grateful that I stopped and he said so several times. The fact that someone stopped—at least one of the hundreds of motorists who passed by—he was given hope, if only for a few minutes, that the road is not such an impersonal, uncaring place after all. We can never overestimate the power of hope.

Max and Rose Schindler tell their riveting story about surviving the Holocaust. Both were sent to concentrations camps as part of the Nazi effort to exterminate Jews. Their stories (told separately until they met after the war in England) are powerful testimonies of the power of hope. The subtitle of their book *Keeping Hope Alive While Surviving the Holocaust* summarizes how they were able to survive the horrific, inhumane treatments to which they were subjected. No human-driven event has caused more despair, hopelessness, and human tragedy than the Holocaust.

Max tells of one event that helped him keep hope alive and it confirms the power of compassion in the face of danger. Late in his experience of the Nazi genocidal program, when he was forced to move to a new camp because the Allies were closing in on the Nazis, Max was the unexpected recipient of kindness from a stranger:

> "The food here is better than camp, but still not enough to sustain us. Men are weak and thin, sickly and have difficulty completing their jobs. There is a civilian German man here, the only one in all the places I have been during the war, who feels any concern for me. He sneaks me bread from his home.

This man is putting his life and mine at risk by giving me bread. We are very careful that no guards are watching when he hands it to me. I am dumbfounded by his courage and kindness."[53]

The unknown German civilian probably never thought about the parable of the Good Samaritan, yet he played the role perfectly. As a result, one man lived longer than he should have and remembered long enough to tell the story. Now, the model of a vulnerable, risk-taking, compassionate stranger serving another stranger in desperate need continues to inspire us.

Someone asked the anthropologist Margaret Mead (1901-1978), "What is the first sign you look for to tell you of an ancient civilization?"[54] The interviewer had in mind a tool or article of clothing. Ms. Mead surprised him by answering, a "healed femur." She explained that when someone breaks a femur, he can't survive to hunt, fish or escape enemies unless he has help from someone else. Thus, a healed femur indicates that someone else helped the injured one rather than abandoning him and saving themselves.

Isn't that what serving is about? Healing femurs of one sort or another? Stopping to help a stranger even when he's not someone we would usually include in our comfort zone? Giving bread to a starving prisoner? Risking our own safety when others are in need? That's the mark of a true compassionary.

---

53 M. Lee Connolly. *Two Who Survived: Keeping Hope Alive While Surviving the Holocaust*. MRS Publishing: San Diego, CA, 2019. p. 109.

54 https://skeptics.stackexchange.com/questions/47543/did-margaret-mead-say-that-a-healed-femur-is-the-earliest-sign-of-civilization, accessed June 5, 2021.

A HEART WITH EYES

.

The Arizona desert is no place to be stranded. It's hot and desolate and unforgiving of poor planning. Novella and Jackie, wife and husband, have lived in the desert long enough to learn those important lessons. When they travel, they always have a supply of food and water, especially water. It can be a long way between places to stop in the desert.

On one of their trips, they stopped at an isolated rest stop and saw an elderly couple having car trouble. The woman was trying to talk to her husband, but he was unresponsive. They were on their way from San Diego to Ohio and had been on the road for four hours when car trouble disabled them. Novella and Jackie offered to help and discovered the diabetic man needed food. They gave him the food and water they had with them, then drove them sixty miles to a store where they bought more food and a gallon of water for the elderly couple's long journey.

This Good Samaritan couple did what came naturally to them—they stopped on the road to help people who needed help. They were prepared and compassionate. As a result, the stranded couple was able to continue their trip; without Novella and Jackie they might have had a much worse experience.

Novella and Jackie are contemporary Good Samaritans. A long time ago they resolved their questions about the wisdom of stopping to help travelers on the road. As they travel now, they actually look for opportunities to help people. Why this choice when so many are reluctant to get involved with strangers in potentially dangerous situations? "You have to be looking to see people who are hurting. They are all around us, but we normally don't see them. You have to look with your heart," explains Novella.

She and Jackie are people of strong Christian convictions. They understand their relationship with Christ as a mandate to serve others any time they have the opportunity. Their joy in serving doesn't just come from being hard-wired to serve; it comes from a sense of calling to do the right thing.

The willingness to serve regardless of circumstances also comes from Novella's childhood, growing up in a large, poor family. "My mamma had ten children and didn't want any of us," she says. "I remember the Lion's Club giving each of us an orange for Christmas and that was our total Christmas. I have never forgotten what it felt like for someone who didn't know me to do something nice for me just because they cared. And I want to do the same for others."

A young woman paced beside her car on the side of the road. She was crying. The raised car hood signaled to anyone who happened to look that she needed help. Novella and Jackie stopped, of course. Others passed by. Novella and Jackie had to stop. It was their calling. Novella comforted the young woman while Jackie assessed her trouble. Jackie didn't have what was needed to do the job so he called a mechanic friend who came from the other side of town to help. Jackie bought the needed part and his friend installed it. He also slipped Jackie a twenty and told him to give it to the young woman for gas; she was sitting on empty. The young woman was effusive in her gratitude. Not only was her car repaired at no cost to her, but her outlook on life was also buoyed by her divine appointment of compassionate help.

Novella and Jackie are well aware that others question the risks they take to help strangers on the road. They are not naïve about the risks, but are committed to push through any concerns they may have to do what they can to help. "Our Lord had compassion on us, and we must respond with compassion to others," says Novella. She and Jackie have hearts with eyes.

PART FOUR

Chapter Ten

COME ON IN. THE WATER'S FINE.

Be of service. Whether you make yourself
available to a friend or co-worker, or you make
time every month to do volunteer work, there is nothing
that harvests more of a feeling of empowerment
than being of service to someone in need.
--GILLIAN ANDERSON

We can get creative when we need to give a reason for not doing something we know perfectly well we should do. For example, a well-known religious leader asked church leaders through Twitter what they had heard from parishioners as reasons for not attending church.[55] Here are some of the more interesting "reasons" they heard:

"We were out of peanut butter."

"Both of my girlfriends attend there."

"The worship leader pulls up his pants too often. It's distracting."

---

55 https://www.churchanswers.com/fifteen-reasons-people-give-for-not-attending-church/April 26, 2017, accessed June, 2021

"The pastor is too attractive. When I see him preaching, I have impure thoughts, and I'm distracted."

"We got burned out on church and have been taking a break the past seven years."

"I always get hemorrhoids on Sundays."

"I was constipated."

As entertaining and ridiculous as these "reasons" are, they show that it's pretty easy to justify our choices for not doing something we would otherwise agree is a good thing to do. The same is true for serving. Most people agree that serving others in need is a good thing--as many as ninety percent of Americans believe that—yet the actual percentage of people involved in serving is closer to twenty-five percent. Furthermore, the benefits of serving are well known, but that doesn't seem to provide much of a boost to the ranks of those who serve. Let's look at the most common reasons people give for not serving and offer a response for each one.

"I DON'T HAVE ENOUGH TIME."

The most common reason for not serving is the lack of time. About half of Americans cite this as the main reason.[56] What's interesting about this is retirees (who presumably have enough time) are less likely to serve than people who work and people aged 35 to 44 (when young children are at home and adults are working).[57] Does this surprise you? One expla-

---

56Amy Yotopoulos "Three Reasons Why People Don't Volunteer, and What Can Be Done About It." https://longevity.stanford.edu/three-reasons-why-people-dont-volunteer-and-what-can-be-done-about-it/, Accessed May 25, 2021.

57 Yotopoulos

PEOPLE WHO SERVE PRIOR TO RETIREMENT ARE TWICE AS LIKELY TO SERVE AFTER THEY RETIRE. A PATTERN OF SERVING BEGINS EARLIER IN LIFE THAT IS CARRIED ON IN RETIREMENT YEARS . . . BOTH FOR THOSE WHO SERVE AND THOSE WHO DO NOT.

nation is people who serve *prior to retirement* are about twice as likely to serve after they retire. Apparently, a pattern of serving begins earlier in life that is carried on in retirement years, both for those who serve and those who do not.

Time is a legitimate issue. Despite forecasts in the latter part of the last century about time-saving technology creating more leisure time than ever, we are in fact busier than ever. As one who is classified as retired, I can testify that what I heard about retirement being as busy as non-retirement is absolutely true. Our perceived shortage of time does not cease to be an issue in serving once a person begins receiving Social Security.

I know what it is like not to serve because I think I don't have enough time. Weeks and months have come and gone while my intention to do hands-on serving was not acted on. I just couldn't seem to find the time. And yet, I have as much time as anyone else—24 hours in a day—but I tend to fill my days with responsibilities or things I enjoy. Only when I made a commitment to seek a regular time and place to serve people in need did I begin to include regular serving in my day-to-day schedule. Would that work for you, too?

A group of Princeton Seminary professors conducted an unusual experiment to see students' response to time and serving someone in need. They divided the students into two groups and told both groups to prepare a talk on the parable of the Good Samaritan (not a coincidence) to be presented later in the day. Then they arranged for a man who appeared to be in trouble—bent over, coughing, unkempt—to be on a bench on the way the students would go to the appointed place to give their talk. The professors told one group they had plenty of time to get to their appointment and the other group they were running late and to hurry. Of those who thought they were late for their appointment, *only ten percent* of them stopped to see if they could help the man on the bench. Of those who believed they had plenty of time, *sixty-three percent* stopped. Having enough time mattered more than preparing for ministry or preparing to talk to others about the Good Samaritan.

I doubt many readers will find the outcome of this experiment terribly surprising. Time may be our most precious commodity, more than money for most of us. If you are not serving now or seldom served in the past because you believe you do not have the time, I offer a couple of suggestions that may help.

Have you assumed that larger blocks of time are required? Not necessarily. If you are able to carve out a block of time regularly to serve, good for you. You will find it rewarding and you will make a difference. But smaller amounts of time are also important. International charity OXFAM[58] got serious about helping people find very small pieces of time in which to serve when they posed the question *What can you do in five minutes?* How would you answer?

---

58 OXFAM is a confederation of 20 charitable organization focused on the alleviation of global poverty. For more information go to www.oxfam.org

- Can you listen to a colleague at work share about a problem at home or work?

- Can you pick up a few things for a disabled or elderly neighbor while you are grocery shopping for yourself?

- Can you pray for your server or salesperson if they share a need for prayer?

- Can you make flyers telling neighbors you are collecting non-perishable goods for a local food pantry (collecting and delivering the goods will require more time)?

- Can you write a hand-written note of encouragement to a person in prison or to a first-responder?

- Can you take food (extra from one of your regular meals) to a neighbor who is temporarily unable to cook his own meals?

- Can you make a couple of phone calls on behalf of a local charity asking people to consider making a donation?

Serving people in need doesn't have to take a lot of time. The important thing is not the amount of time devoted to serving or even what you do but doing it for the right reason—to meet a real need when you see it. One small step with a short-term task may inspire you to find more time, either additional short segments or a larger opportunity to serve. No one has ever said it better than Mother Teresa, "It is not how much you do, but how much love you put in the doing."

Next, review your schedule to see if there might be small pockets of time that could be used in serving. Often when someone says she doesn't have time to serve, she is thinking about her entire schedule and how harried she feels trying to accomplish all her responsibilities. For most of us, however, a busy schedule doesn't mean that every waking moment is booked. We have smaller amounts of time--an hour or two, that could be used for a meaningful activity. That's part of the equation of solving the time crunch. Time spent serving is rewarding and meaningful, it gives you a sense of purpose and makes you happy. If your schedule is crammed with responsibilities, some of which are rather mundane, wouldn't it be a welcome change if some of that time were given to serving

> "IT IS NOT HOW MUCH YOU DO, BUT HOW MUCH LOVE YOU PUT IN THE DOING."
>
> —MOTHER TERESA

others? Wouldn't it be beneficial for your mental and spiritual health to find some time—not every day or even every week-- to help people who cannot do for themselves?

"I DON'T KNOW WHERE TO START."

I have heard this reason for years, especially from people who have not served very much. Essentially, this translates to, "I don't know where I fit in serving" or "I don't know how to find the right opportunity for me" or "I'm not opposed to serving, but I am at a loss as to know how to begin." Some uncertainty is due to the novelty of a new situation, just as with anything else we do for the first time. I remember the first time I attempted snow skiing. I didn't grow up in an area where there was enough snow to ski and my family couldn't afford it, so I was a middle-aged adult before I tried skiing. When I climbed into the boots and clicked into the skis the first time (with a great deal of help from a friend), I felt awkward, even anxious. I didn't know what to expect and I didn't know how to stay upright on the slick snow. When I saw others on the slopes, it looked like fun, but I felt more apprehension than excitement.

Before you wade into serving, unfamiliarity can create feelings of anxiety and awkwardness, but these can be overcome. A good way to get past these feelings is to remember something you did for the first time, how you felt about that and how, once you did it a few times, those feelings faded. Unfamiliarity was replaced with familiarity. Uncertainty was replaced with comfortable expectations. The first time you sat behind the wheel of a car probably felt a little strange or scary. You were responsible to make the car go where you wanted it to go, to safely navigate traffic, to handle all the responsibilities that come with operating a motor vehicle which you had probably taken for granted because someone else was driving. But your desire to drive without depending on others helped you push past your concerns. Soon, your confidence in driving rose and your concerns melted away.

This may sound elementary and an oversimplification for your apprehension of serving, but it works. The process of becoming comfortable with a new behavior can work for serving just as it has for hundreds of other behaviors in your life. This simple, common sense approach can be a good first step in overcoming any apprehensions you may feel about serving people in need.

WHAT IF I GET INTO A SITUATION I AM NOT PREPARED TO DEAL WITH?

Whether or not you have experience in serving others in need, it is common to be concerned that serving can lead to deeper involvement in the lives of those being served. Anticipating this development can make you pause even before you start.

Let's look at a real-world example. You serve your colleagues at work by listening to their personal problems when they need to talk to someone they trust and over a period of time you hear a colleague pour out her heart about an abusive relationship with her husband. You do your best to comfort and encourage her, but when she leaves her husband, fearful of what he will do, and asks if she can stay with you temporarily, you are torn between offering her sanctuary and protecting your family from possible dangers. "This is not what I signed up for" may be your first thought. "What do I do now?" Each person in a situation like this must come to his own decision as to what to do.

Here are some options: You can agree to allow your friend to stay with you and your family for a short time until she is able to make other arrangements, but this decision must involve your family. They need to know the facts and be aware of possible consequences of a troubled friend taking refuge in your home. You can refer your friend to a shelter that houses women in cases of domestic violence. Such shelters protect their residents and are equipped to help them start a new life. Both of these options are serving. Both are sincere and compassionate.

I offer a rule of serving here that applies to many different and unforeseen circumstances: Know your boundaries. Be clear with yourself and (if the need arises) with those you serve about what you can and cannot do. It is one thing to put yourself "out there"; it is something else entirely when serving leads to the unexpected involvement of others who may not have agreed to be part of what you are doing. The vast majority of serving does not involve this sort of risk. Serve whenever and wherever you can and be wise and prayerful about how deeply you get involved in another's life.

WHY SHOULD I HELP PEOPLE WHO WON'T HELP THEMSELVES?

Some people have made a conscious decision not to serve people in need because they question whether those people are actually needy. They may believe so-called needy folk have created their own crises and want others to come to their rescue. They may have a set of unspoken criteria for helping that prevents them from getting involved in certain situations. Fred Craddock, venerable and popular Methodist preacher of the recent past, told about his student pastorate in a small church. The church had an Emergency Fund with about $100. Church leaders told him that, as pastor, he could use the money to help people at his own discretion, provided he dispensed the money according to certain conditions. "What are the conditions?" he asked. He was told, "You are not to give the money to anybody who is in need as a result of laziness, drunkenness, or poor management." Craddock quipped in retelling of the story, "Far as I now, they still have that money."[59]

In serving people in need, it is easy to become skeptical and judgmental. Most people who have not experienced actual hunger, homelessness, or situations of real poverty lack understanding of circumstances that lead to those needs. From a "have" position, "have-nots" sometimes appear to be victims

---

59 Brian's Lines: The Pastor's Helper. Richardson, TX: From the Ministry of Brian L. Harbour. March/April, 2002, p. 24.

of their own bad decisions. With this sort of judgmental attitude it is difficult to feel the compassion that leads to serving.

In the town where I live, a non-profit offers training in
understanding the causes and circumstances of poverty. Participants go through the typical day of a poor person who
cannot get a job that pays better than minimum wage, who
has no transportation, who may have children who require
care while the parent works taking a sizable chunk of their
income. When these people are sick, they miss work and do
not get paid for time lost; if that sickness lasts long enough
(and they may have no health care so there are new expenses),
they may lose their job and their income and their home, and
suddenly they are homeless, unemployed, unhealthy, and out
of options. There are more people than we realize who are one
paycheck away from the streets.

There are also people who are victims of their own bad
judgment or addictions. Serving these people is more chal-
lenging as the line between helpful and harmful is blurred. So,
what are we to do? How do we deal with the destructive behavior we may face in those we work with from time to time?
How do we handle our desire to back away from these people?
Here are a few suggestions to deal with this real and persistent
obstacle to serving:

1. Avoid a blanket policy that treats all people the same. All
   people are not the same and all circumstances are not the
   same. Take each person, each situation of need as unique
   and worthy of careful examination. Within the scope of
   what is possible, try to discern a person's needs and how
   he can be served.

2. Strive to be helpful, not harmful. Saying no to a presenting need may be hard, but it may also be the right thing to do.

3. Err on the side of compassion. It's not always easy to know what is helpful and what is harmful. Serving is seldom black-and-white; there is a whole lot of grey. In that greyness, I encourage you to err on the side of kindness.

"NO ONE ASKED ME TO."

One out of four people say they don't volunteer because no one asked them to.[60] I can't explain this, but I know it's true. Rather than speculate as to the basis of this reasoning, I prefer to point out the benefits of serving in hopes that inspiration will trump reluctance. If you are one waiting to be asked to serve people in need, please consider how you can help with little investment of your time. When you serve others, you give them hope for a better future. You help them see that someone cares. When you serve people in need, you contribute to the alleviation of their needs and hurts. When you serve people in need, you make your community a better place to live. Like the person who has jumped into a lake beckoning others to follow by saying, "Come on in; the water's fine," I say, "Come on into serving; you'll be ever so glad you did."

One church organized a day of service in their community, but when the event was proposed to the congregation, it did not get immediate approval. One man voiced his opposition saying that it was a waste of time and money, the church had better things to do. But the congregation approved the effort

---

60 Yotopoulos

and planning moved forward. To his credit, the outspoken opponent signed up to participate in the project that served coffee to drivers at a nearby truck stop. As he served, he learned about the hardships of being a trucker and experienced firsthand the value of doing something as simple as giving a cup of coffee. He enjoyed serving so much that he went back the next few months on his own to serve coffee to the truckers! Another reluctant soul was drawn into the role of serving despite his misgivings and quickly became another compassionary.

Chapter Eleven

WHAT'S THAT IN YOUR HAND?

The place God calls you to is the place where your
deep gladness and the world's deep hunger meet.
--FREDERICK BUECHNER

One of my favorite Bible stories is Moses' calling by God to liberate the people of Israel from Egypt. Moses was a shepherd in the land of Midian having married into a farming family. He came to Midian fleeing Egypt after killing an Egyptian soldier. One day, while tending sheep, he saw a bush on fire which was strange because no one else was around. Even stranger was the fact that the bush did not burn up. So, Moses went to investigate this fiery bush. When he came close to the bush, God spoke to him. As if a burning bush wasn't scary enough, God's voice must have terrified him, but what God said was even scarier. He told Moses to go to Egypt and lead the Israelites out of Egypt to the land he had promised their ancestors. This was truly *Mission Impossible* for Moses. In the first place, Moses was just a shepherd with no leadership or military experience. To think he was qualified to do what God told him to do was crazy. In the second place, the people of Israel were slaves to the Egyptian nation and the Pharaoh was not about to let them leave without a fight. Moses wasn't up for a fight in a land he had fled in fear for his life.

When Moses objected to God's instructions, God asked him, "What's that in your hand Moses?" Of course, Moses was holding his shepherd's staff. It was the primary tool he used in his job as a shepherd. God told him to throw the staff on the ground and when Moses did, the staff turned into a snake. Moses was afraid. Then God told Moses to pick up the snake—to take it by the tail and pick it up. When Moses did that, the snake became a staff again. God did this to show Moses that he was serious about giving him the job of liberating his people from Egypt and that he would make sure Moses could fulfill that calling regardless of his doubts or lack of experience.

Earlier, we talked about serving as a calling. Now, let's look at how I believe God equips us to fulfill that calling, maybe not in such a miraculous way as he did for Moses. If reading this book has opened you to the possibility of serving, then I would not be responsible if I didn't try to help you find an experience of serving that suits you. How can you find a place to serve that fits you?

YOUR SWEET SPOT

In *The Externally Focused Church*, Rick Rusaw and Eric Swanson introduce a model for helping a congregation find where they can serve most effectively in their community. Their model suggests that a church's sweet spot of serving is the intersection of their community's needs and dreams, the mandates and desires of God, and the calling and capacities of the church.[61] Picture three overlapping circles: one circle represents the needs and desires of the community, one the mandates and desires of God, and one the calling and capacities of the church (figure 1 below). The church's sweet spot of service is where the three overlap. The model works for individuals, too. The first two circles are the same and the third is the calling and capacities of the individual (figure 2).

Let's look at the first two circles. The needs and desires of the community refer to the needs of people who are unable to provide for themselves and the community's dreams of the best they can be.

Figure 1

---

61 Rick Rusaw and Eric Swanson, *The Externally Focused Church.* Group Publishing, 2004, pp. 52-74.

These needs may be identified in a study of needs conducted by city officials or local non-profits. They may include homelessness, poverty, hunger, disability, aging, and other locally identified needs. (See Appendix A for more information on how to locate your community's needs.)

The second circle refers to God's desire to care for the poor and marginalized and the example of Jesus in serving people in need throughout his public ministry. (Appendix C lists prominent biblical passages that spell out God's desires and expectations regarding compassion ministry.) These two realms—the needs of the community and the desires of God--are external to the person serving. In the process of finding your place of serving I encourage you to investigate these two areas of necessary information.

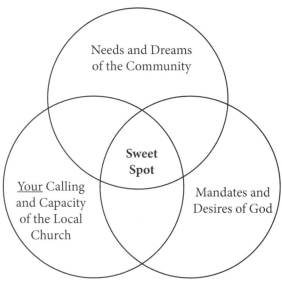

Figure 2

Next, I want to help you to discover your sense of calling and your capacities for serving. These are unique to you; they belong to no one else. They may be similar to the capacities of others, but these are yours. Learning about these unique aspects of your personal experience will help you discover your sweet spot for serving.

BEGIN AT THE BEGINNING

Keep in mind that an opportunity for serving is not like a position of employment. Your education, specialized qualifications, training, and experience are not the necessary criteria for serving although what you bring to the table may help you find your place of serving. Remember, serving people in need does not require any particular skill set or training (which is not to say you can't serve more effectively with training or some expertise). Anyone can serve. Availability is what matters.

The factors that make up your calling and capacities for serving are your life experiences, your passions, and the needs available and attractive to you. Not everyone starts serving from the same place. Some of us were introduced to serving by our upbringing. We were fortunate to have serving modeled for us by our parents and other influential adults so that the desire to serve is in our DNA. We just need an opportunity. Others begin at zero—little if any experience with serving. From where do you begin? If you have experience in serving, is there something about that experience that gives you a clue as to where and/or how you should serve now?

I am a great believer in how our past provides guidance for our future. In my own life, I have seen that where I am headed is usually a continuation of where I have been perhaps with a few new twists and turns. For example, if you have previously been involved in helping the homeless, especially during your formative years, you may have a special feeling for the homeless due to that experience. That special feeling may be the seed of your passion for the homeless which indicates a good place to begin (or continue) serving.

Try this simple process to help you focus on your place to serve. Make a list of all the ways in the past when you have served people in need. Don't leave anything out, no matter how far back it goes or how small it is. Circle the ones that gave you the most joy. Finally, narrow the list down to your top three. Then see if one of these three rises to the top in areas of serving that you are drawn to.

What if you have almost no experience in serving? Look at the experiences or seasons of your life in which you encountered some sort of pain. One person writing about serving explains, "Your pain is your purpose."[62] He means we are best motivated to serve others when we want to help those who struggle with the same painful experiences we have had.

Maxine Raines found herself on the streets at the tender age of six when her alcoholic father jumped on a freight train and never came back. Her schizophrenic mother could no longer take care of Maxine and her younger brother, so Maxine lived on the streets from age six to fifteen. Then she lied about her age to get married to a thirty-two-year-old man she hardly knew. The marriage didn't last long, and Maxine made her way back to her hometown. Years passed; Maxine learned how to get by on her own and eventually, she became an LPN, able to provide for herself. Her years on the street cultivated a

---

62 Evan Carmichael, *Built to Serve*. New York: Savio Republic Books, 2020, p. 137.

deep compassion for the homeless. She *knew* their struggles. She *knew* their pains. Eventually, she felt God pulling that compassion and experience together to call her to launch a ministry to the homeless in her hometown. Lost Sheep Ministry is a vibrant support of the homeless in Knoxville, Tennessee even though Maxine has retired from its leadership.[63]

Personal pain can be a strong indicator of how we should serve others. To be able to say honestly to another person who is struggling "I know how you feel--I've been there" is gold. But I have also seen people equally motivated by needs they encounter that have nothing to do with their own story. One woman helped upgrade the playground at a school that doesn't get much attention from the community or the school district because it serves low-income students. While she was there, it occurred to her that some of the students might need help learning to read so she spoke with the principal and was soon assigned to work with several students who were reading far below grade level. She didn't just read books from the school library. She wrote stories about her own life which the students enjoyed much more. Her mentoring of the students grew out of her exposure to the needs of the school and the students it served. (If you are interested in

OPPORTUNITIES TO SERVE PEOPLE IN NEED DO NOT HAVE TO BE PLANNED; THEY CAN BE SPONTANEOUS. BUT FOR THAT TO HAPPEN, THERE HAS TO BE A SERVING MINDSET IN PLACE.

---

63 Richard Briggs, *Maxine: A Woman's Remarkable Walk With God.* Createspace Publishing, 2015.

using some of the tools available to help you discover your passions and life experiences to find an ongoing place of service, go to Appendix B. There is a list of resources designed to help you identify what you have to offer in experience and skill and how your interests and passions may match service opportunities.)

EVERYDAY SERVING

Serving people in need is more about the heart than the head. The stimuli for serving spring from humility, seeing needs, compassion, courage and responsibility more than a well-designed process for finding your passion and purpose. Opportunities to serve people in need do not have to be planned; they can be spontaneous. But for that to happen, there has to be a serving mindset in place. This is not to say a thoughtful assessment of your life experiences and passions are not helpful; they are, but you can serve every day in small ways that are unexpected and unplanned. I want to affirm any attempt to serve people in need whether planned or unplanned, big or small, long-term or temporary. Louise Jackson, an eighty-nine-year-old volunteer with Foster Grandparent, sums it up, "Step-up, get-up, show-up, listen-up, and grow-up."[64]

What do you hold in your hand today? Your life experiences and passions will help you locate where and how you can serve well. Moses did go back to Egypt and eventually persuaded Pharaoh to allow the people of Israel to leave. When they had journeyed only a short distance, they came to the

---

64 Barbara R. Metzler. *Passionaries: Turning Compassion Into Action.* Philadelphia: Templeton Foundation Press, 2006, p. 51.

Red Sea with no way to get across. Moses lifted up the staff-become-snake-become-staff-again and the sea parted, and the people walked across on dry land. When they had spent time in the wilderness and their water supply ran dangerously low, Moses struck a rock with the staff-become-snake-become-staff-again and water poured forth to quench the people's thirst. When they were attacked by the Amalekites, Moses held up the staff-become-snake-become-staff-again for the duration of the battle and God gave them a victory. When we give God what he has put in our hand, he gives it back to us, but it's different. It may appear to be the same, but it is infused with divine power—the power of serving!

What's that in your hand?

Chapter Twelve

SEE A NEED, MEET A NEED

"You must be the change you wish to see in the world."
--GHANDI

Have you seen the movie *Pay It Forward*? It is the delightful if somewhat tragic story about a middle school teacher and his seventh-grade student who accepts the challenge to think of an idea that has the potential to change the world and to put his idea into action. The student comes up with the idea of "paying it forward"—doing something to change the life of three people for the good, asking them not to pay him back, but to "pay it forward" by helping three other people. Then those three do the same for three more people, multiplying somewhat random acts of compassion. Three becomes nine, nine becomes twenty-seven, then eighty-one, and on and on until the impact is felt throughout the world. At first, the young boy is frustrated as it appears that none of the people he helps is really changed, but by the end of the movie, it is clear that his simple idea has indeed changed the world as reports come in of people "paying it forward." The success of the movie is not in how many people saw it or how much money it grossed, although it did well at the box office, but in the fact that its title has become a universal phrase for helping people in need.

Would that it could happen that way! Would that the idea of serving people in need would become so popular that it would be commonplace to see people serving others—spontaneously, willingly, happily, individually and collectively. Would that serving others would become so widespread that it is the rule rather than the exception. Would that serving others would become so trendy that it would be hard to find needs not being met.

It can be. Serving can change the world. Change of this magnitude won't happen suddenly because masses of people start behaving differently than they do now. Change will come when *individuals* begin behaving differently, who influence other individuals to behave differently, who inspire others to act differently, who continue to pay it forward. The concept may be the basis of a sweet and hopeful movie, but the methodology is sound. It's called multiplication. The principle of multiplication is at work constantly—in the fads and trends that gain traction in large numbers. Why can't it work with serving others?

We all know what compound interest is—the multiplication of interest upon interest so that even a fairly meager investment grows faster than appears possible. For example, an investment of just $100 at 4 percent interest will grow to $222.26 in 20 years without any additional investment. An investment of $1000 at 5 percent interest will be $2,712.64 in 20 years. Why not "compound serving"—one person building on another's service, both building on those results until hundreds or thousands of volunteers would be serving people in need? One person would become two, say, in a month and four people in two months and sixteen in three months, and more than four million in just six months! It can happen. The math makes it sustainable if the chain of compounding remains intact.

This is what it comes down to: one person at a time deciding to make serving part of his daily routine, sharing his experiences and encouraging others to do the same, celebrating the positive outcomes. Then the process is repeated when the next person does the same. Over time, the world is changed-- one compassionary at a time.

Let's review.

We are hard-wired to serve others. Our brains are equipped to stimulate service with feelings of pleasure and reward when we serve.

We are called to serve others. God wants us to give ourselves to others, especially those who cannot help themselves. Jesus made serving others the highest calling.

Serving others gives us hope. It gives hope to those around us and especially to those whom we serve. Hope encourages people in need to do what they can to help themselves.

Serving builds community and has the potential to break down deep divisions in our communities, bringing us together with our neighbors.

Serving does not require special skills or training. Anyone can serve, even the most limited among us.

Opportunities to serve are everywhere—from the homeless shelter in your town to the elderly neighbor down the street, from the bold organization fighting sex trafficking to the children in your community's schools who are falling behind.

So, what about it? Will you be a compassionary? Will you make serving part of your daily routine? Will you be a link in the multiplication process with the understanding that your impact will go far beyond you, perhaps throughout the world? I continue to be inspired by the grandmother (mentioned in a prior chapter) who refused to let her age, or anything else keep her from doing what she could to make her community a better place to live, to lift up her neighbors. Her motto, "step-up, get-up, show-up, listen-up, and grow-up," gives us an outline for what it takes to become a compassionary.

STEP UP: GET OFF THE SIDELINES AND INTO THE GAME.

The world needs more people serving, for several reasons. First, there are more needs than there are people working to meet them, so plenty of needs go unmet every day, every year. Second, the world needs more people with a serving attitude. We need to change the prevailing attitude of "what's-in-it-for-me?" The world needs people who are more concerned about others than about themselves. We need people who will step up.

Thirty-eight million people (11.8%) in the U.S. live in poverty. (World Vision defines poverty as an income of less than $33.26 per day or less than $12,000 per year for an individual.) In 2018, the USDA reported that 11.1 percent of U.S. households were food insecure, meaning they have difficulty providing sufficient food for their family. Seventeen out of every ten thousand (or 567,715) people in the U.S. are homeless. These statistics are but a tiny sample of the needs that exist today and the needs continue to grow.

These statistics are overwhelming, maybe even paralyzing for some of us. Instead of inspiring us to reduce these numbers, we throw up our hands in frustration wondering where to begin. That's understandable, but you are not responsible for world hunger. You are responsible to address hunger that persists in your community or neighborhood. Even Jeff Bezos or Warren Buffett can't solve the problem of *world* hunger alone. This is what needs to happen: See A need, meet A need.

You may say, "What can I do? I am just one person." Consider the power of one. One person can influence masses given the right circumstances. One person—not necessarily a powerful person-- can start a movement. Rosa Parks became the face of the Civil Rights Movement when she refused to sit at the back of the city bus in Montgomery, Alabama, but did you know there was someone who came before Rosa Parks who inspired her to do what she did? Claudette Colvin, a fifteen-year-old black girl, was riding a city bus in Montgomery in March, 1955. She and her friends were told to move to the back of the bus to make room for a white woman. All of Colvin's friends moved back but she stayed put and was arrested. One person inspired another person who inspired a movement that has changed America.

> I AM ONLY ONE, BUT I AM ONE. I CANNOT DO EVERYTHING, BUT I CAN DO SOMETHING. I WILL NOT LET WHAT I CANNOT DO INTERFERE WITH WHAT I CAN DO. AND BY THE GRACE OF GOD, I WILL.
>
> —EDWARD EVERETT HALE

Nancy Lawlor collects bouquets—flowers from hotels, weddings, and corporate events, in cities like New York and Los

Angeles. Then she gives them away to people in need, often breaking down larger bouquets so there's more to go around.

Lawlor was inspired to start her nonprofit organization, FlowerPower, eight years ago. Sitting in the lobby of the Waldorf Astoria, she was riveted by its towering floral displays. "Where did they go at the end of the day?" she wondered. After getting her answer—a dumpster—Lawlor volunteered to take them away instead. Once the hotel agreed, Lawlor delivered $2,000 worth of large pink bouquets to a New York City hospital. "It all started with one person saying yes," she says. To date, FlowerPower has distributed more than $2.5 million worth of flowers to hospitals, rape crisis centers, and rehabilitation clinics. The bouquets last several days, giving patients a healthy dose of good cheer. "I've seen thousands of people transformed," she says, "all over a simple bouquet of flowers that originally would've been thrown away." Now, that's a beautiful arrangement.[65]

Steve Jobs said, "The people who are crazy enough to think they can change the world are the ones who do." Are you "crazy enough" to become a compassionary?

GET UP: STAND UP FOR THE PRIORITY OF SERVING.

Serving needs advocates, people who will recruit others to serve, people who recognize the potential of serving to solve problems and create authentic community. Be outspoken. Take advantage of every opportunity to remind your peers of the transformational power of serving.

65 https://www.rd.com/article/the-power-of-flowers-nancy-lawlor/ Accessed June 8, 2021.

As a minister, I naturally think of the church when I think of enlisting others in serving. You may think serving is endemic to church life, but you would be mistaken. The *Pareto Principle*—20 percent of the people do 80 percent of the work—is as true for church as anywhere else. Church participants are just as likely to substitute giving money for hands-on service as anyone else. They are just as likely to believe they are too busy to serve. If you attend a church, speak up about the need for *everyone* to be involved in serving people in need. Jesus set a clear example of serving and his followers also are to serve.

If you are not a churchgoer, recruit your friends, family, and neighbors to get involved in serving. Share what serving means to you and how you serve. Invite them to join you. Your reasons for serving may differ from those who do so as part of their faith but what you do helps meet needs as much as anyone's service. Compassionaries are missionary-like in how they draw others into serving.

SHOW UP: SEIZE THE OPPORTUNITY TO SERVE OTHERS.

Lily Tomlin said, "I always wondered why somebody doesn't do something about that. Then I realized I was somebody." You are a compassionary when you see a need and meet it, or at least try to meet it. You do not wait for someone else to do it. You show up to do it yourself. Showing up is taking responsibility. Actually, it's better than that—it's taking advantage of an opportunity to be the change you want to see. A sense of responsibility is a good thing. It helps us act when faced with a need.

Even better is seeing the need of another person as an opportunity to serve. When we encounter a person in need, it's an opportunity not only to provide the help but also to fulfill our calling to serve, another chance to experience the benefit of serving, another opportunity to be a positive example of serving for passers-by. Who wouldn't want to do that? So, is it a responsibility or an opportunity? Yes.

LISTEN UP: BELIEVE IN THE POWER OF SERVING.

Serving is one of the most powerful forces in this world. It confounds the eloquent and silences the arrogant. It soothes the angry and heals multitudes of pains. It brings people together and binds them into community.

One of the secrets of the power of serving is its contagion. Serving tends to spread. One of the most amazing examples of the contagion of serving took place in the drive-through at a popular fast food restaurant. One customer paid for the order of the driver behind him. That customer paid for the next order as well, and the next paid for the next and so on. In all *288 consecutive customers paid for the orders of those behind them in the drive-through line!* Is that not powerful?

But serving has to have method of delivery. It's like a fresh water lake that has the potential to sustain a nearby town but without the pump and pipes to deliver the water, it is only a potential resource. Serving needs people like you and me to be its delivery system. There is no other way. Compassionaries are convinced about the power of serving. They see themselves as the pipeline of service delivering its therapeutic powers where they are needed. Margaret Mead once said, "Never believe that a few caring people can't change the world. For, indeed, that's all who ever have."[66]

Jesus turned this world upside down. He showed that what the world thought was weakness was in fact strength. He demonstrated that worldly power is ineffective when he allowed himself to be executed by his enemies. His resurrection stands as an eternal statement about worldly power and real power. When he wrapped himself in a towel, poured water in a basin and stooped to wash the disciples' feet, he showed the power of serving. And the world has not been the same since.

GROW UP: GROW YOUR CAPACITY FOR COMPASSION.

Compassion grows with use. Compassion is not used up. It is not a finite resource; if I share out of my sense of compassion I don't have less. The more we exercise compassion, the more it grows. The more we exercise compassion in serving others, the greater our capacity for compassion becomes.

Compassion is a spiritual muscle. Athletes grow muscles by using them, actually straining them to their limits while training them to do what they want them to do. Athletes' muscles are not depleted when they exercise; they grow stronger and bigger. This is how it is with compassion: it grows with use. So, the more you exercise compassion in serving others, the more it will grow and the more you will want to use it

---

66 https://www.google.com/search?q=quotes+by+margaret+mead&rlz=1C-1CHBF_enUS829US829&oq=quotes+by+margaret+mead&aqs=-chrome..69i57j0i22i30.5165j1j15&sourceid=chrome&ie=UTF-8 Accessed June 8, 2021.

again and again. Compassionaries enjoy an ever-growing capacity for compassion.

FINALLY, SERVE UP: UNLEASH THE POWER OF SERVING

Some readers may still wonder if serving is really powerful even though we have tried to clearly outline the benefits to those who serve as well as those being served and to the larger community. It seems so simple, so unexciting, so routine.

Think of the process of nuclear fission. It is the result of splitting an atom, producing vast, immediate energy. An atom is not visible to the naked eye, yet we know it's there. It has several parts--protons, electrons and neutrons. Nuclear fission happens when a neutron, travelling at just the right speed, is shot at an atom's nucleus. The nucleus splits and energy is released. When a nucleus is split under the right conditions, some stray neutrons are also released, and these neutrons can split other atoms, and these additional split atoms can split other atoms creating a chain reaction. When a single atom is split, the energy produced is miniscule. But when the chain reaction of fission occurs in less than a second, an enormous amount of energy is produced—enough to destroy entire cities with an atomic bomb or enough to produce electricity for an entire city. We live in the age of nuclear energy and enjoy its benefits (as well as the apprehension that this power can be used for evil purposes). While the average person may not understand how it works, he nevertheless accepts the fact that nuclear energy is real and powerful.

Serving is also powerful. It has the power to change a person's heart forever. It has the power to transform neighborhoods and communities into places of good will and mutual caring. It has the power to raise an individual from despair to hope. It has the power to heal broken relationships.

Nuclear power is more powerful than originally expected. The key to nuclear power has been learning to harness the energy produced for constructive purposes. Serving power is also greater than we think. Who can measure the value of personal transformation or community transformation? Who can say what the ultimate impact will be when a small group of people decide to make serving part of their everyday lives so that it happens frequently and naturally? No one would have guessed that building one house for one family in Americus, Georgia would grow into an international organization changing the lives of thousands of people in need of housing, harnessing the efforts of millions of volunteers who work with Habitat for Humanity. No one could have predicted that a slight, unknown woman from Albania would influence generations of people to be more compassionate and to serve people in need as Mother Teresa did.

Serving can change the world! We need people who want to change the world, ordinary folks like you and me with a serving mentality. We need compassionaries who make serving their mission. Are you willing to sign up?

30 DAY CHALLENGE

1. Read and commit to memory *The Compassionary's Pledge* at the end of this book. This is a personal commitment, maybe to God or maybe to your community, that serving people in need will become a way of life for you. Every day for 30 days, repeat this pledge to yourself. Make it part of your morning routine like showering or

dressing for the day. *When* you say it is not as important as that you do it. If you are a person of faith, you may want to make it a prayer.

2. Throughout each day ask yourself, *Is there someone I can serve? Is there a need I can meet today?* Watch and listen for answers. As a reminder, place a tiny dot on the face of your watch or your phone so that you see it every time you look at it throughout the day.

3. Make a game out of your system of remembering to serve others. Keep score—give yourself a point when you do something in the way of serving. Use stickers as a reward and challenge yourself to get thirty stickers in thirty days, or use marbles, moving one marble each time you participate in some act of serving, working toward your goal of filling a container with thirty marbles in thirty days.

4. Test the results of serving described in this book. See if serving even in the simplest way makes you happy. See if serving grows your capacity for compassion. See if serving strengthens your relationships. Do this part of the challenge at least once a week during these 30 days.

5. Share what you are doing with your family and friends. Stand back and watch what happens. Watch the power of serving remake your world!

You can do this! We can do this! Let's do it together.

COMPASSIONARY PLEDGE

As a citizen of this world, I pledge to be a compassionary by answering the high calling to serve people in need.

I promise to keep my eyes and heart open today to the needs of others and seize the opportunity to serve them.

I promise to respect people in need as I offer them help and hope.

I promise to listen to their hurts and hopes and act accordingly.

I promise to be wise and compassionate in how I serve others.

I promise to make myself available throughout the day to the ways I might be used to serve those around me.

Appendix A

HOW TO FIND NEEDS IN YOUR COMMUNITY

Whereas *Compassionaries* calls all of its readers to serve people in need, some may be unsure how to get started. This appendix is intended to jump start that process. Chapter 11 speaks of one's "sweet spot of serving" which is the intersection of God's mandates to serve people in need, your passions and capacities for serving and the needs of the community. The average person is not well informed about how to find human needs, so Appendix A offers additional information about how to find needs in the community.

Larger communities often have a sort of catalogue of local needs available. This valuable resource brings together into one place information about most if not all types of needs and the churches, agencies and non-profits serving those needs. Usually, this resource can be found in local government offices, particularly community development or Community Action Council and public library. If your community has such a resource, that is a good place to start in locating a place you may serve.

It may be helpful to begin by identifying one or two categories of needs to which you feel some attraction. I have listed below some categories of needs and common ways these needs are addressed in a community. You will see that each category describes how that type of need manifests itself, the specific needs therein and typical sources where information about that category may be found.

DISABILITY

--Manifests primarily as mobility/strength issues but may also produce other needs due to limited income such as food insecurity, assistance for daily routines

--Needs may include wheelchair ramp, grab bars for bathroom, door openings, person(s) to provide physical assistance

--Sources of information:
- Veteran services including American Legion, VA hospitals
- American Association for People with Disabilities
- American Council for the Blind
- National Association of the Deaf
- The Arc (intellectual and development issues)
- Local Disability Service agencies

SHELTER

--Manifests as homelessness, safety in cases of domestic violence, victims of fire or natural disaster, loss of housing by unwed expectant women

--Needs center around adequate shelter, usually temporary. Needs go beyond shelter to include compassion for victims of domestic violence, disaster and unwed mothers. Once shelter is provided, volunteers are needed to respond to emotional needs of victims.

--Sources of information:
- International Hospitality Network
- Family Promise Ministries
- Salvation Army
- Local homeless shelters

CHILDREN

--Manifests as safety in cases of physical and/or emotional abuse, hunger, poor academic opportunities/performance and poverty which often produces health issues and other needs

--Needs may be shelter/adequate home environment in cases of abandonment or foster care, health care, ongoing need for nutritious food, safety in cases of abuse, tutoring and/or mentoring

--Sources of information:
- Boys and Girls Club
- Schools (teachers know the needs of their students)
- Foster Care/Adoption agency
- Local agencies focused on children's needs

FOOD

--Manifests as hunger or food insecurity (uncertainty where next meal will come from), occasional health issues from inadequate nutrition

--Needs are availability/distribution of food

--Sources of information:

- Food pantries (many of which are operated by churches)
- Food bank (larger operation than food pantries, often supplying food to pantries)
- Mobile Meals (Meals on Wheels usually operated out of a local government agency)
- Schools

IMMIGRANTS/REFUGEES

--Manifests as shelter, assimilation into a new country/community, unemployment, enrollment in schools, childcare

--Needs are housing (temporary then permanent), help with language, employment, schooling for children and other childcare, access to government services, language education (ESL classes)

--Sources of information:

- Bridge Refugee Services
- Welcome House
- Office of Refugee Resettlement (U.S. Dept. of HHS)

POVERTY

--Manifests as low income which produces a range of needs, unemployment, food insecurity

--Needs are inadequate housing, inadequate food, clothing, health care, unemployment

--Sources of information:
- Local benevolent agencies which may provide food, clothing, assistance with utilities/rent (often supported by churches as well as other non-profit organizations)
- Employment agencies
- Employment counseling agencies

HEALTH

--Manifests as chronic disease(s), nutritional issues, inability to obtain necessary medications

--Needs are access to health care providers, transportation, financial help with medications

--Sources of information:
- Local non-profit health clinic(s)
- Local Health Department
- U.S. Department of Health and Human Services

HOUSING

--Manifests as inadequate or unsafe housing

--Needs are new housing, repairs to existing housing, assistance with rent and/or application for subsidized housing

--Sources of information:

- Habitat for Humanity
- Local Community Development Department
- National Low Income Housing Coalition
- Children's Bureau: U.S. Department of Health and Human Services

Appendix B

TOOLS FOR FINDING YOUR SWEET SPOT IN SERVING

Chapter 11 talks about finding your sweet spot in serving. One of the keys in that process is identifying your capacities for serving which come from experiences, talents and passions. This appendix offers information about some tools that can aid in the process of clarifying your capacities for service. Rather than offering a one-size-fits-all process, the information provided here is meant to facilitate your personal search for your capacities. When the information garnered by using one or more of these tools is combined with the information in Appendices A (How to Find Needs in Your Community) and C (Biblical Passages Exposing God's Heart for People in Need), clarity should emerge regarding a good fit for serving.

FINDING YOUR PASSION

If you Google "how to find your passion," you will get 30 million results in .9 seconds (really!). Who has time to check out all those results? I have spent a some time looking at a number of the results that showed up under these key words and listed below a few that appear to me to be worth a look. Bear in mind that most articles and books on finding one's purpose/passion/strengths come at this from the career perspective, not serving people in need as a volunteer. However, discovering your passion will inform your search for your "sweet spot in serving."

Online article: "Five Steps to Finding Your Passion" by Susan Haas. Psychologytoday.com, May 8, 2012

Online article: "How to Find Your Passion" by Ken Coleman. Ramseysolutions.com/career-advice/how-to-find-your-passion. June 22, 2021

Online article: "How to Find Your Passion: 7 Steps You Can Take Today" by Jules Schroeder forbes.com/julesschroeder/2017/06/15/how-to-find-your-passion-sh=225e2258615f

The Passion Test: The Effortless Path to Discovering Your Destiny by Janet Bray Attwood and Chris Attwood is a popular book on finding one's passions and learning how to live in them. While the book does not speak about serving people in need directly, the process of discovery of passions can be helpful in identifying ways of serving that match up well with one's passions and lead to fulfilling service. The book is an easy and entertaining read with step-by-step instructions.

RESOURCES FOR FINDING YOUR STRENGTHS

Cliftonstrengths 2.0 is a popular tool for identifying your strengths. Over 25 million have used it. This tool has been developed by the Gallup organization and offers numerous additional tools to help a person apply the outcomes of the assessment in finding suitable places to work and serve. The assessment has a small fee and takes about an hour to complete.

The High5 Test at *high5test.com* is a free resource that has also been used by millions to identify their strengths and offers additional resources by which to apply the findings for a good fit to serve and work.

Forbes published a helpful article in 2018 in which 15 of their coaches offer their favorite tool in finding one's strengths and weaknesses: "Best Tests To Help You Understand Your Strengths and Weaknesses." The list includes such standards as SWOT, DISC, EQ Assessment as well as a number of others. The value of the article is its gathering of information about assessing strengths and weakness in one place. Readers can make an informed choice as to which tools to investigate further and perhaps utilize. Access this article at: https://www. forbes.com/sites/forbescoachescouncil/2018/01/22/best-tests-to-help-you-understand-your-strengths-and-weak-nesses/?sh=461db506495a

ONLINE RESOURCES FOR VOLUNTEERING

"How To Find the Ideal Place to Volunteer" by Kerry Hannon (Forbes, May 11, 2016) is one of many, many articles to be found online offering help for anyone who prefers to conduct some research on serving before jumping in. This article offers common sense suggestions as to what one should take into consideration when deciding how and where to serve.

An amazing online resource for locating non-profits and other organizations or agencies where you may serve people in need is Volunteer Match: *volunteermatch.com*. The site shows plenty of places in your locale that need volunteers. You can search by category of need or by organization or by skills required to serve. This site does not offer help in identifying a person's capabilities or passions to serve. Similar online sites that offer help for volunteering are *Idealist.org* and *Handson-network.org*.

Appendix C

BIBLE PASSAGES FOR SERVING PEOPLE IN NEED

OLD TESTAMENT

"Do not mistreat an alien or oppress him, for you were aliens in Egypt." Exodus 22:21

"Do not take advantage of the widow or an orphan. If you do and they cry out to me, I will certainly hear their cry." Exodus 22:22-23

"Do not deny justice to your poor people in their lawsuits." Exodus 23:6

"When you reap the harvest of your land, do not reap to the very edges of your field or gather the gleanings of your harvest. Leave them for the poor and the alien. I am the Lord your God." Leviticus 23:22

"For the Lord your God is God of gods and Lord of lords, the great God, mighty and awesome, who shows no partiality and accepts no bribes. He defends the cause of the fatherless and the widow, and loves the alien, giving him food and clothing. And you are to love those who are aliens, for you yourselves were aliens in Egypt." Deuteronomy 10:17-19

"For there will never cease to be poor in the land. Therefore, I command you, 'You shall open wide your hand to your brother, to the needy and to the poor, in your land.'" Deuteronomy 15:11

"He raises the poor from the dust and lifts the needy from the ash heap; he seats them with princes and has them inherit a throne of honor. For the foundation of the earth are the Lord's upon them he has set the world." 1 Samuel 2:8

"Whoever heard me spoke well of me, and those who saw me commended me, because I rescued the poor who cried for help, and the fatherless who had none to assist him. The man who was dying blessed me; I made the widow's heart sing." Job 29:11-13

"[God] shows no partiality to princes and does not favor the rich over the poor, for they are all the work of his hands." Job 34:19

"A father to the fatherless, a defender of widows, is God in his holy dwelling." Psalm 68:5

"How long will you defend the unjust and show partiality to the wicked? Defend the cause of the weak and fatherless; maintain the rights of the poor and oppressed. Rescue the weak and needy; deliver them from the hand of the wicked." Psalm 82:2-4

"I know that the Lord secures justice for the poor and upholds the cause of the needy." Psalm 140:12

"He upholds the cause of the oppressed and gives food to the hungry. The Lord sets prisoners free, the Lord gives sight to the blind, the Lord lifts up those who are bowed down, the Lord loves the righteous." Psalm 146:7-8

"Do not withhold good from those whom it is due when it is in your power to act." Proverbs 3:27

"The poor are shunned even by their neighbors, but the rich have many friends. He who despises his neighbor sins, but blessed is he who is kind to the needy." Proverbs 14:20-21

"When you are generous to the poor, you are enriched with blessings in return." Proverbs 22:9

"The generous will themselves be blessed, for they share their food with the poor." Proverbs 22:9

"Open your mouth for the mute, for the rights of all who are destitute. Open your mouth, judge righteously, defend the rights of the poor and needy." Proverbs 31:8-9

"Feed the hungry, and help those in trouble. Then your light will shine out from the darkness, and the darkness around you will be as bright as noon." Isaiah 58:10

"If you really change your ways and your actions and deal with each other justly, if you do not oppress the alien, the fatherless or the widow and do not shed innocent blood in this place, and if you do not follow other gods to your own hard, then I will let you live in this place, in the land I gave your forefathers for ever and ever." Jeremiah 7:5-7

"You trample on the poor and force him to give you grain. Therefore, though you have built stone mansions, you will not live in them; though you have planted lush vineyards, you will not drink their wine. For I know how many are your offenses and how great your sins. You oppress the righteous and take bribes and you deprive the poor of justice in the courts." Amos 5:11-12

"This is what the Lord Almighty says: 'Administer true justice; show mercy and compassion to one another. Do not oppress the widow or the fatherless, the alien or the poor. In your hearts do not think evil of each other.'" Zechariah 7:9-10

NEW TESTAMENT

"Learn to generously share what you have with those who ask for help, and don't close your heart to the one who comes to borrow from you." Matthew 5:42

"So, when you give to the needy, do not announce it with trumpets, as the hypocrites do in the synagogues and on the streets, to be honored by men. I tell you the truth, they have received their reward in full. But when you give to the needy, do not let your left hand know what your right hand is doing." Matthew 6:2-3

"Jesus answered, 'If you want to be perfect, go, sell your possessions and give to the poor, and you will have treasure in heaven. Then come, follow me.'" Matthew 19:21

"Then the King will say to those on his right, 'Come, you who are blessed by my Father; take your inheritance, the kingdom prepared for you since the creation of the world. For I was hungry, and you gave me something to eat, I was thirsty and you gave me something to drink, I was a stranger and you invited me in, I needed clothes and you clothed me, I was sick and you looked after me, I was in prison and you came to visit me.'

"'Then the righteous will answer him, 'Lord, when did we see you hungry and feed you, or thirsty and give your something to drink? When did we see you a stranger and invite you in, or needing clothes and clothe you? When did we see you sick or in prison and go to visit you?'

"The King will reply, "I tell you the truth, inasmuch as you did it for one of the least of these brothers of mine, you did it for me.'" Matthew 25:34-40

"He went to Nazareth, where he had been brought up, and on the Sabbath day we went into the synagogue, as was his custom. And he stood up to read. The scroll of the prophet

Isaiah was handed to him. Unrolling it, he found the place where it is written: "The Spirit of the Lord is on me, because he has anointed me to preach good news to the poor. He has sent me to proclaim freedom for the prisoners and recovery of sight for the blind, to release the oppressed, to proclaim the year of the Lord's favor." Luke 4:16-19

"For even the Son of Man did not come expecting to be served by everyone, but to serve everyone, and to give his life as a ransom for the salvation of many." Mark 10:45

"Cornelius, God has heard your prayer and remembered your gifts to the poor." Acts 10:31

"Let each of you look not only to his own interests but also to the interests of others." Philippians 2:4

"If any woman who is a believer has widows in her family, she should help them and not let the church be burdened with them, so that the church can help those widows who are really in need." 1 Timothy 5:16

"Do not forget to do good and to share with others, for with such sacrifices, God is pleased." Hebrews 13:16

"Little children, let us not love in word or talk but in deed and in truth." 1 John 3:18

"Religion that God our Father accepts as pure and faultless is this: to look after orphans and widows in their distress and to keep oneself from being polluted by the world." James 1:27

"What good is it, my brothers, if a man claims to have faith but has no deeds? Can such faith save him? Suppose a brother or sister is without clothes and daily food. If one of you says to him, 'Go, I wish you well; keep warm and well fed,' but does nothing about his physical needs, what good is it?" James 2:14-16

"Each of you should use whatever gift you have received to serve others as faithful stewards of God's grace in its various forms." 1 Peter 4:10

ABOUT OPERATION INASMUCH

Operation Inasmuch began in 1995 at Snyder Memorial Baptist Church, Fayetteville, North Carolina. It is a model of community ministry in which an average of 60-70 percent of a congregation's average attendance is mobilized throughout their community to minister to people in need. This is a one-day blitz conducting a variety of hands-on projects and engaging all ages groups in ministry to the least, the lonely and the lost.

In 2007, David Crocker launched Operation Inasmuch, Inc., a faith-based, non-profit ministry to share the Inasmuch model to as many congregations and other groups as possible. Since then as many as 2,300 congregations in 25 states and 4 other countries have conducted Inasmuch events. One of the most significant such events took place in April of 2008 when about 1,100 churches covering all 100 counties of North Carolina did an Inasmuch Day. The last 4 years (pre-pandemic) saw an average of 21,500 volunteers mobilized to conduct 2,413 ministry projects in 396 churches in 15 states (and 1 foreign country) serving 198,018 people in need generating $3,113,960 in value of service.

The Inasmuch ministry has developed 2 major expansions of the one-day blitz: (1) Inasmuch United—many churches, one day—a multi-church, multi-racial, multi-denominational ministry event and (2) Lifestyle Compassion Ministry—one church, many days—ongoing compassion ministry that engages believers in year-round ministry building meaningful relationships and transforming individuals and entire congregations.

For more information about Operation Inasmuch, check out their website: www.operationinasmuch.org

ABOUT THE AUTHOR

 David Crocker was a senior pastor of churches in several states for 30 years. In 2007 he launched the faith-based, non-profit Operation Inasmuch, Inc. through which he has equipped over 2,300 congregations in 25 states and 4 countries with the Inasmuch model of compassion ministry. The amazing growth of this model has been the impetus for David's passion for serving. (See About Operation Inasmuch on the next page.)

David describes his life journey as picking up steam instead of slowing down in his later years. There is more work to be done. His passion for serving has only grown in recent years as he continues to dream and work toward seeing serving become a major movement in the world. He says: "This is possible as people self-identify as *compassionaries* and embrace that role as their calling."

David is blessed with a large, loving family. His son and daughter and two step-daughters have given him and his wife,

Brenda, 10 grandchildren. He enjoys woodworking, biking, and reading . . . and ice cream though he has taken a break from that delight for a while! *Compassionaries* is David's third book. *Operation Inasmuch: Mobilizing Believers Beyond the Walls of the Church* (2005) and *The Samaritan Way: Lifestyle Compassion Ministry* (2008) were written as resources for the Inasmuch ministry.

For more information about David and *Compassionaries: Unleash the Power of Serving*, including a Study Guide and online course, blog and other features go to his website: www. davidwcrocker.com .

ACKNOWLEDGEMENTS

Writing a book is never a solo accomplishment. There are folk who are directly—editors, readers, publishers, etc.--and indirectly involved—inspirers, bloggers and authors of other books and articles furnishing valuable knowledge and stories, and people who support the enterprise with their prayers and money. I am incredibly blessed to have a wealth of both direct and indirect involvement in this undertaking. A great deal of the value this book may be deemed to have is due to their participation. I will not attempt to name each one, but some deserve public appreciation for their part in this gratifying process.

A host of people associated with the Inasmuch ministry have made this book possible by their faithfulness to the work of the ministry and by the way they have made serving people in need a lifestyle. I am especially grateful for the encouragement of the staff—Gene Whaley, Bobbie Jo Mitchell and Janice Emge—and the Board of Directors for their unhindered support of this project.

Shane Crabtree of Christian Book Services has been extremely valuable and a completely accessible resource throughout the publishing process. It is hard to imagine a better publisher to work with in publishing a book. They truly put the author first in their approach to the business of book publishing.

From the outset, it was my intention to write a book to stimulate conversations among as many people as possible about serving including believers and non-believers. I was convinced the best way to reach as many people as possible was to get the book out there quickly and inexpensively. A good number of friends have made this possible with their financial support—about 50 of them. Several are due special thanks for their generosity: Jim and LaVerne Craig, Doug and Jane Young, Vicki Williams, and Larry Bass.

Editor Gina Austin was a Godsend. I did not know her until I was almost finished writing the book and somewhat stumbled onto her as an editor. Her expertise and perspective on a book of this kind was enormously valuable in molding the book into a form that not only makes it more readable but also more attractive all readers.

Any author who truly wants to reach others with his message recognizes the need to have people other than himself read and offer helpful feedback on his material. I have been blessed to have several people to do that for me. First readers and long-time friends Jim and LaVerne Craig, Susanne Burnette, Vicki Williams, Bryan Wilson and Bob Bales have done that work with honesty and encouragement. I have also benefitted from a writing coach, Mary Lou Reid, who has consistently offered expert advice and encouragement in writing a book of this kind.

Sharing a personal story is . . . , well, personal. Those who told their stories of serving others so I could include them in this book—what I call stand-alone stories—were reluctant because they do not serve in order to receive praise or recognition. I have changed their names to honor this concern, so I will not name them here, but I want to say a special Thank You to each of them for sharing, but more so for inspiring unknown numbers of readers of their stories.

Finally, I am grateful for a partner in life who shares my passion for serving others and throughout the process of writing participated in reviewing what I wrote, design of the cover and some of the research. Most importantly, she has been a constant source of encouragement and support in ways only a wife can do. Thank you, Brenda, for believing in me and demonstrating that belief in so many ways.